SIMPLE SOMATIC THERAPY FOR TEENS

CONQUER ANXIETY, DEPRESSION, AND TRAUMA, MASTER
EMOTIONAL INTELLIGENCE, AND STRENGTHEN CONFIDENCE AND
RELATIONSHIPS IN JUST 10 MINUTES A DAY

HOLISTIC HARMONY PUBLICATIONS

Holistic Harmony
Publications

CONTENTS

MASTER YOUR EMOTIONS & TAKE CONTROL

Don't wait—grab your workbook now and start owning your emotions today!

Scan QR Code to grab your FREE worksheets:

FOREWORD TO SIMPLE SOMATIC THERAPY FOR TEENS

Welcome to *Simple Somatic Therapy for Teens*, a guide designed to help you explore the powerful connection between your body and mind. Whether you're facing stress, anxiety, self-doubt, or simply navigating the complexities of adolescence, this book offers you tools to tune into the signals your body is sending and learn how to use them as a source of strength, healing, and growth.

As a teen, you are already experiencing a period of rapid physical and emotional change. These transitions can sometimes feel overwhelming or confusing, and you might find yourself feeling disconnected or out of control. This sense of disconnection is common, especially when entering treatment or therapy. It's easy to feel like things are happening *to* you rather than *with* you, and that your body, mind, and emotions are working against each other. But somatic therapy invites you to flip this narrative—to realize that your body is not something to fight against, but a powerful ally in your healing journey.

Through years of working with adolescents in inpatient treatment centers, I have witnessed firsthand how traditional talk therapy alone is not always enough to help young people navigate the complexities of their emotions. Some of the most transformative moments in therapy have come not from words but from movement, breathwork, and grounding exercises that allow teens to connect with their bodies in a way that fosters healing from the inside out. Somatic therapy helps regulate the nervous system, break free from trauma patterns, and empower teens to reclaim control over their emotional and physical well-being.

This book provides an accessible, step-by-step approach to integrating somatic techniques into everyday life. Whether you're struggling with test anxiety, emotional shutdown, trauma, or an overwhelming sense of stress, the exercises and strategies in this book offer practical, immediate ways to regulate emotions and restore balance. You don't need a clinical setting, a therapy session, or years of specialized training to use these tools—they can be practiced anywhere, whether before an exam, in the middle of a stressful social situation, or at home when emotions feel unmanageable.

This book is not about "fixing" anything, but about discovering how you can support yourself in moments of difficulty. Through guided exercises, journal prompts, and creative activities, you will build an awareness of how emotions show up in your body and how you can work with them rather than against them. You'll also learn techniques to manage stress, increase emotional intelligence, and foster a deeper connection to your own needs and desires.

Healing is not linear, and growth takes time. Approach these exercises with patience, curiosity, and compassion for yourself. There's no "right" way to do this work—what matters most is that you begin where you are and honor your journey.

Whether you use this book on your own or with the support of a trusted adult or therapist, know that the tools you are about to explore have the potential to help you create lasting, positive change. *Simple Somatic Therapy for Teens* is more than just a collection of exercises—it's a roadmap to empowerment, resilience, and self-awareness.

You are worthy of the healing that awaits. Let this be the start of your journey toward a more embodied, empowered version of you.

With warmth and encouragement,

Melissa Ginest, MA LPC

Specialist in Adolescent Mental Health & Trauma Recovery

INTRODUCTION

"Your body hears everything your mind says."

— NAOMI JUDD

Imagine this scenario: Laila, a teenage girl, sits in her room feeling overwhelmed by the demands of friends, social media, and school. Her breathing is shallow, her chest feels tight, and her mind is racing with worries she can't seem to shake. She might look like any other teen scrolling through her phone, but inside, she's struggling.

One day, Laila tries something new: She places her hand on her heart and takes slow, deep breaths. For the first time in weeks, she feels calm. That small change sparks her curiosity, leading her to explore somatic therapy—a practice that helps her reconnect with her body, process her emotions, and take back control of her life. As Laila practices, she feels more confident, less stressed, and better equipped to face her challenges.

If you've ever felt like Laila, navigating the pressures of school, friendships, and life as a teenager, this book is for you.

As a mental health provider with years of experience working with teens, I've seen firsthand how transformative somatic therapy can be. I've watched teens go from feeling completely overwhelmed by anxiety to finding clarity and calm through simple, body-centered techniques. I'm passionate about sharing these tools because I know how much they can help.

Growing up, I saw the impact untreated stress and trauma had on my peers—and even on myself. If I had known about somatic therapy back then, my journey would have been different. That's why I wrote this book—to give you access to tools that can truly make a difference.

Somatic therapy is about understanding how your mind and body work together. It's based on the idea that emotions and past experiences aren't just stored in your head—they're also held in your body. By focusing on things like movement, breathing, and body awareness, somatic therapy helps you release stress, process emotions, and feel more balanced. The best part? It's practical, easy to use, and flexible enough to fit into your everyday life.

Being a teen today is tough. Nearly one in five teens struggle with mental health challenges like anxiety, depression, or trauma. Social media, school stress, and leftover impacts from the pandemic only make things more complicated. That's why you need tools that actually work, and somatic therapy is one of them. It gives you a way to manage stress, feel better, and take control of your mental health.

This book is your guide to handling the hard stuff life throws at you. Whether you're feeling overwhelmed by emotions, struggling with stress, or trying to heal from past trauma, somatic therapy can help. The book is designed to give you the tools to feel more in control, face challenges confidently, and bounce back stronger when life gets tough.

Inside, you'll find simple exercises to help you tackle stress, manage anxiety, and better understand your emotions. These practices will help you handle whatever comes your way by building emotional strength and making you feel more balanced. You'll also learn step-by-step techniques you can use anytime, anywhere, and tips for boosting your confidence and resilience.

This book is for teens who want to take charge of their emotions, parents who wish to support their kids, and counselors looking for practical tools that make a real difference. While it's geared toward teen girls, the exercises and advice are adaptable for anyone ready to feel calmer, stronger, and more in control.

This isn't just a book—it's a guide to building a better relationship with your emotions. Dive into the exercises, reflect on what works for you, and explore how somatic therapy can help you thrive. Life may be complicated, but you can navigate it confidently and clearly with the right tools. Ready? Let's get started!

1

UNDERSTANDING SOMATIC THERAPY

"Even when words fail, your body still speaks. Somatic therapy gives that voice a safe place to be heard."

— HOLISTIC HEALING CONCEPT

E mma, a second-year high school student, is holding her notecards for an important history presentation as she stands outside her classroom. Her heart is racing, her throat feels constricted, and her palms sweat. She is gripped by her anxiety of speaking in front of her peers. "What if" scenarios are racing through her head: What if I forget everything? What if they laugh?

But instead of letting the fear take over, Emma remembers something her counselor taught her. She puts her feet firmly on the ground and inhales deeply. She visualizes herself being steadied by roots that grow from her soles into the ground. She puts her palm on her stomach, takes a steady breath, counts to four, and then lets it out again. In a matter of seconds, the constriction in her chest starts to loosen up, and she feels enough at ease to enter the room and make her presentation.

Emma could transition from panic to poise by focusing on her body and grounding herself. Somatic therapy's main goal is for one to learn to tune into one's body to manage stress, process emotions, and find balance.

WHAT EXACTLY IS SOMATIC THERAPY?

Somatic therapy is about using your body to understand and manage your emotions. The word "somatic" comes from the Greek word for "body," and that's exactly what this approach focuses on—tapping into the wisdom stored in your physical self. It's based on the idea that your mind and body are totally connected, like a team, with your emotions showing up in your body and your body influencing how you feel. Cool, right?

Somatic therapy takes a different approach to mental health. Instead of just talking things out like in regular therapy, it focuses on how your body reacts to stress, anxiety, and feeling overwhelmed. Think about it—do your shoulders tense up? Does your chest feel tight? Do you get that sinking feeling in your stomach? Somatic therapy helps you notice these signs and understand what's going on inside. Even better, it teaches you simple techniques to chill out and feel balanced again.

Somatic therapy uses simple but powerful techniques like deep breathing, grounding, and gentle movements to help you reconnect with your body. For example, focusing on your breath can calm a busy mind, while slow, intentional movements can help you release pent-up emotions. These are tools that, over time, can train your body to handle stress in a healthier, more balanced way.

Somatic therapy is amazing because it's simple and fits right into your daily life. Whether you're stressed out, cramming for an exam, or coping with a tough breakup, somatic techniques can give you instant relief while also helping you build long-term emotional strength.

THE ORIGINS & EVOLUTION OF SOMATIC THERAPY

Somatic therapy is built on an idea that's been around forever: Your mind and body are deeply connected. Cultures worldwide have known for centuries that mental and physical health go hand in hand. Yoga, meditation, and traditional practices like Chinese medicine and Ayurveda have always emphasized listening to your body to create balance and harmony. These ancient methods laid the groundwork for today's mind-body healing techniques.

Fast forward to modern times, where pioneers like Wilhelm Reich—one of Sigmund Freud's students—helped kick things off by exploring how emotions are stored in the body. He even coined "body armor" to describe the physical tension caused by bottled-up feelings. Later, innovators like Peter Levine, who developed Somatic Experiencing, and Alexander Lowen, the founder of bioenergetics, took these ideas further (Admin 2024). They introduced ways to use movement and body awareness to release stress and heal from trauma. Levine's work, for example, showed how focusing on the nervous system can help you feel safer and more connected after challenging experiences.

Somatic therapy is still evolving, blending ancient wisdom with modern psychology and neuroscience. It's recognized as an effective tool for managing everyday stress and healing deep emotional wounds. Combining the best of old and new, somatic therapy offers practical, effective ways to grow, heal, and thrive.

THE SCIENCE OF THE MIND-BODY CONNECTION

Your mind and body are always in conversation, shaping how you feel and respond to the world. This connection becomes super obvious when you're stressed out. Ever notice your shoulders tighten up when you're anxious or how your heart races before a tough talk with a friend? These are signs of how closely your mental and physical states are linked.

Inside your brain, little chemical messengers called neurotransmitters are working hard to control your mood, energy, and focus. When everything's in balance, you feel calm, steady, and ready to handle anything. But when life throws stress or emotional challenges your way, that balance can get thrown off. If serotonin dips, you might feel down or irritable. If dopamine is out of whack, concentrating can feel impossible. The good news? Somatic therapy can help. It supports your body's natural balance, calms your nervous system, and makes you feel grounded again.

Stress is another way your mind and body talk to each other, and let's be honest—it can get LOUD. When you're stressed, your body goes into fight-or-flight mode. Your breathing gets faster, your heart races, and stress chemicals like cortisol flood your system. It's your body's way of protecting you in emergencies, but if stress sticks around too long, it can leave you drained and exhausted. Somatic therapy can quiet that stress response. Simple techniques like grounding or focusing on your breath can teach your body to chill even when things get intense (Harvard Health 2024).

Trauma cranks up this mind-body connection even more. Even if your mind wants to move on after a challenging experience, your body might still hold on. A particular sound or situation might make your stomach churn, or your chest tighten, even if you're unsure why. This is your body remembering the trauma. Somatic therapy helps you gently work through these reactions, releasing tension and helping you feel safe again.

Even depression doesn't just stay in your head—it shows up in your body, too. You might feel heavy, exhausted, or stuck, like everything takes extra effort. Depression can make it hard to feel connected to your body at all. Somatic therapy uses small but powerful practices like movement, breathwork, or tuning into your sensations to help you reconnect. These steps can help you feel more alive and present, little by little.

Your body plays a huge role in healing. By listening to what it's telling you and using somatic techniques, you can go beyond just managing symptoms—you can create real balance and calm from the inside out. Somatic therapy isn't about "fixing" you. It gives you tools to feel better and stronger in a way that works for *you*.

WHY YOU NEED SOMATIC THERAPY

Being a teenager today is more demanding than ever. You're facing challenges that weren't as intense for previous generations. Social media, school stress, and figuring out who you are can leave you feeling overwhelmed, anxious, or unsure of yourself. That's where somatic therapy comes in—it helps you build self-awareness, resilience, and the tools you need to handle life's ups and downs confidently.

The Pressures You Face Today

Social media has altered teenagers' interactions with the outside world, and not always in a positive way. Your self-esteem may suffer significantly due to the ongoing pressure to maintain the "right" experiences, look perfect, and stay updated with ongoing comparisons. In addition, you feel pressured to perform well in extracurricular activities and schoolwork to stay up with the times. Then there's the inner work of being a teen: figuring out who you are, who you want to be, and how you fit in.

These stressors manifest not just in the mind but also in the body. You may have a knot in your stomach when contemplating going to a school function or stress in your chest before sharing a picture online. By addressing these physical sensations, somatic therapy gives you the tools to relax mentally and physically when life feels too much.

SOMATIC VS. TRADITIONAL TALK THERAPY

Traditional therapy, often referred to as talk therapy or psychotherapy, is a broad term that includes different approaches to help people address mental health challenges. These types of therapy have been developed over time to meet various needs, and they all share the goal of exploring your thoughts, feelings, and behaviors to promote understanding and personal growth. Cognitive behavioral therapy (CBT) focuses on identifying and changing negative thought patterns, while psychodynamic therapy examines how unconscious thoughts influence your actions. Humanistic therapy emphasizes self-growth and reaching your potential, and dialectical

behavior therapy (DBT) blends mindfulness
with techniques to manage intense emotions and build coping skills. Each approach provides unique tools and perspectives to help you navigate challenges and improve your mental well-being.

While traditional therapy works well for many, it often focuses more on your thoughts and emotions and less on how stress or trauma shows up in your body. This is where somatic therapy stands out, as it addresses the connection between your mind and body. In somatic therapy, you learn to notice how your body reacts to experiences. For instance, a therapist might ask, "What do you feel in your body when you think about this?" They may also observe your posture, movements, or physical responses, helping you connect your emotions to what's happening in your body.

Somatic therapy uses techniques that go beyond talking. Body awareness helps you recognize physical sensations tied to emotions. Gestures and movement allow you to process feelings through physical expression. Breathwork calms your nervous system, while light touch can promote relaxation and ease tension. Somatic therapy creates a more balanced and complete healing experience by working with your mind and body.

Limitations of Traditional Approaches

Traditional talk therapy has helped many people better understand their thoughts, feelings, and actions. However, it doesn't always address the physical side of stress, anxiety, or trauma. These experiences aren't just mental—they show up in your body as tight shoulders, a knotted stomach, or a racing heart. Talk therapy can help you understand why you're stressed, but it doesn't always give you the tools to release that tension physically.

Somatic therapy fills this gap by using techniques like grounding, body scans, and gentle movement to help you let go of what's weighing you down. It also shines in the moment when emotions are intense. While talk therapy focuses on reframing negative thoughts, somatic techniques like deep breathing help calm your nervous system immediately, relieving you when you need it most.

Combining somatic therapy with traditional therapy creates a complete approach. If you're anxious, talk therapy can help you explore the root of your worries, while somatic techniques like breathwork can calm your body in the moment. Together, these methods build long-term emotional and physical resilience, helping you feel more balanced and capable.

Integration Somatic Therapy With Other Methods

Somatic therapy is powerful on its own, but combining it with traditional talk therapy can create a holistic approach to healing. Imagine being stuck in talk therapy, reliving a painful experience without feeling any relief. Adding somatic techniques like grounding or gentle movement can help you reconnect with your body and release the tension tied to those emotions. It's like hitting a reset button on your nervous system, making it easier to process your experiences fully and move forward.

By blending somatic therapy with talk therapy, you bridge the gap between thoughts and feelings. For example, talk therapy might help you understand patterns like feeling unworthy, while somatic therapy helps you notice physical reactions, like tight shoulders, tied to those feelings. Combining mindful stretches or breathing exercises with cognitive work creates a synergy that enables you to break harmful patterns more effectively.

This integration lets you think through your challenges and feel your way through them, leading to a deeper and more lasting sense of healing. It's a practical way to handle emotional and physical stress while honoring the connection between your body and mind.

REAL-LIFE APPLICATIONS AND BENEFITS

Let's discuss how somatic therapy can improve your life. Whether you're struggling with stress, anxiety, sadness, or even trauma, this approach offers valuable tools to improve your physical and mental well-being.

Easing Stress

Let's say you've had a difficult day. You may have missed an assignment deadline, been fighting with a friend, or felt overburdened. Not only does that stress remain in your mind, but it also accumulates throughout your body, causing headaches, tense shoulders, and a tight jaw.

Somatic therapy is like hitting the reset button for your body and mind. One simple technique is a quick body scan. Here's how it works: Close your eyes and mentally check in with different parts of your body. Maybe you notice your stomach feels tight or your shoulders are scrunched up. Taking a few deep breaths and focusing on relaxing those spots can help your body let go of the tension it's been holding onto. It's a super easy way to feel calmer and more in control.

Coping With Depression

When you're feeling down, it can feel like your body is stuck in the same rut as your mind. You might feel drained, disconnected, or just numb. Somatic therapy helps you reconnect with yourself in a kind and judgment-free way.

Imagine placing your hand on your heart and taking slow, steady breaths. This small, simple action can help you feel grounded and safe in your body. Over time, these little moments of awareness can create a powerful link between your emotions and how your body feels, making it easier to shake off the heavy weight of depression.

Managing Anxiety

Picture this: You're about to walk into a big exam, and suddenly, your heart's racing, your palms are sweaty, and you feel like you might freeze up. That's anxiety kicking in—your body's way of reacting to danger, even when there isn't any. But guess what? Somatic therapy can help you take back control.

In moments like this, a grounding exercise can work wonders. Try this: Plant your feet firmly on the ground, take a slow, deep breath, and press your palms together. As you exhale, focus on the warmth of your hands or the solid feeling of your feet on the floor. This simple move tells your brain, "Hey, I'm safe," calming your nerves and helping you focus so you can crush that exam.

Healing Trauma

Trauma can leave deep marks on your body, even long after the event. Maybe certain situations tense your muscles, or a sudden loud noise makes your heart race without warning. These are your body's way of holding onto what happened, even if your mind has moved on.

Somatic therapy offers a safe way to work through these reactions. For instance, a therapist might guide you to notice where you feel tension in your body and use calming techniques like deep breathing or gentle movements to release it. Over time, this helps ease those automatic responses, giving your nervous system the chance to heal and reset.

BUILDING RESILIENCE FOR EVERYDAY LIFE

The cool thing about somatic therapy is that it's not just about fixing problems—it's about building resilience and strength to tackle whatever life throws your way. Regularly checking in with your body makes you more self-aware and feel more in control. You'll learn to handle tough emotions confidently and face challenges calmly instead of panicking.

Somatic therapy isn't about being perfect—it's about making progress by finding small, meaningful ways to boost your mental and physical health, one step at a time. Whether you're dealing with intense emotions or need a reset after a rough day, these practices can help. And the best part? You already have everything you need—your breath, your body, and your awareness.

Building Resilience with Somatic Practices

Being resilient doesn't mean avoiding challenges—it means knowing how to handle them when they show up. That's where somatic therapy has your back. Learning techniques like deep breathing or grounding allows you to stay calm and collected even when life gets messy.

For example, if a tough conversation with a friend overwhelms you, you can try a grounding exercise to slow your breathing and quiet your thoughts. Or, after a stressful day at school, a simple movement exercise can help you shake off built-up tension. These small but powerful tools can make a big difference over time, helping you bounce back from life's ups and downs with confidence and ease.

Fostering Self-Awareness & Self-Regulation

Your teenage years are all about figuring yourself out—like understanding why you feel the way you do and learning how to handle those emotions in a healthy way. That's why somatic therapy is perfect for this stage of life. It helps you pay attention to what's happening in your body so you can connect your emotions to your reactions.

For example, if you notice your jaw tightens when you're upset, somatic techniques can teach you how to relax before anger takes over. This kind of self-awareness is a game changer for building emotional maturity and stronger relationships.

Somatic therapy also gives you tools to stay in control. When you're feeling irritated or on edge, you can practice calming techniques to pause, breathe, and respond thoughtfully instead of acting out in the moment. These skills aren't just helpful now—they'll make life easier for years to come.

ADDRESSING OBJECTIONS TO SOMATIC PRACTICES

It's normal to feel skeptical about somatic therapy at first. Focusing on your body might seem strange, or you might wonder if these techniques really work. But many teens and parents have seen how somatic practices can help with stress, anxiety, depression, and trauma. For instance, one of my patients who struggled with severe anxiety found that grounding exercises helped her stay calm during panic attacks. Therapists often highlight how somatic techniques are especially effective for treating trauma, with many teens experiencing breakthroughs that talk therapy alone couldn't provide.

These results are backed by science. Studies show that somatic practices help regulate the nervous system, reduce PTSD symptoms, and build emotional resilience (Kuhfuß et al. 2021). Plus, they're safe and accessible. Techniques like deep breathing and body scans are gentle and flexible, making them easy to try, no matter your experience or physical ability. You can practice them while sitting, lying down, or even moving at your own pace, making somatic therapy approachable for everyone.

Time can also feel like a barrier, especially when life is packed with school, activities, and friends. But somatic therapy doesn't require a huge time commitment. Quick habits, like taking a few deep breaths before a test or doing a grounding exercise during a stressful moment, can fit seamlessly into your day. These practices don't feel like extra tasks—they're simple ways to feel more in control without adding to your to-do list.

Even if you're unsure at first, the benefits of somatic therapy become clear with time. These techniques help you build self-awareness and emotional control, offering instant stress relief and real personal growth. Over time, you'll gain confidence in managing your emotions and feel stronger in all areas of your life. Somatic therapy also tackles the root causes of stress, providing long-term healing and helping you see your own potential. It's a game changer for handling challenges and building resilience.

Time and Commitment

Life as a teen is busy. Finding time for anything extra can feel impossible between school, activities, and hanging out with friends. But somatic therapy doesn't have to take up much of your time. Quick, simple habits like a few minutes of focused breathing or a grounding exercise can easily fit into your schedule. You can even work them into your day, taking deep breaths before a test or paying attention to how your body feels while you walk to class. These techniques are designed to feel natural and doable, not like another thing on your to-do list.

Even if you're skeptical at first, the impact of somatic therapy eventually becomes clear. These practices help you build self-awareness and emotional control, offering instant stress relief and real personal growth. The more you practice, the better you'll get at managing emotions, which boosts your confidence and resilience in all areas of your life.

But the benefits don't stop there. Somatic therapy tackles the root causes of mental and physical stress, leading to long-term healing. It's a total game changer, helping you handle stress in a healthy way and giving you a new perspective on your strength and growth potential.

A MESSAGE FOR PARENTS AND TEACHERS

Parents, guardians, and teachers play a huge role in helping teens navigate their mental health. While guidance from trusted adults often gets the ball rolling, somatic therapy can be a total game changer. By introducing teens to somatic techniques and creating a safe space to explore their emotions, you can set them up with skills they'll use for a lifetime.

Start by leading by example. Teens pick up a lot from watching the adults around them. If they see you using deep breathing to handle stress or grounding yourself during a chaotic moment, they're likelier to give it a shot themselves.

You can also encourage teens to incorporate somatic practices into their daily lives. Suggest a grounding exercise before a big test or help them create a calming nighttime routine. Connect them with resources like mindfulness classes, somatic therapists, or books like this, if possible.

Most importantly, remind them it's okay to feel what they're feeling. The goal of somatic therapy isn't to erase emotions but to help them identify and handle those feelings with confidence and resilience. With your support, teens can build the self-awareness and emotional strength they need to thrive in today's world.

Download your interactive chapter worksheets _NOW_ to apply these techniques, track your progress, and build real emotional resilience—one step at a time.

SCAN QR CODE FOR DOWNLOADABLE WORKSHEETS

INTERACTIVE WORKSHEET

Exploring Your Mental and Physical Goals with Somatic Therapy

Instructions:

Take a few moments to reflect on your personal goals for somatic therapy. Write your answers in the spaces provided. Be as honest and detailed as you can—this is your journey, and these goals will guide you as you explore somatic techniques.

Step 1: Reflect on your current feelings.

1. What are three words that describe how you're feeling mentally right now?

    ◦ _____
    ◦ _____
    ◦ _____

2. What are three words that describe how you're feeling physically right now?

    ◦ _____
    ◦ _____
    ◦ _____

Step 2: Set your mental goals. Think about what you'd like to achieve mentally through somatic therapy.

1. What challenges or struggles would you like to work on?
2. How would you like to feel mentally after practicing somatic techniques?

Step 3: Set your physical goals. Somatic therapy helps connect your mind and body.

1. What physical sensations or issues (like tension, racing heart, etc.) would you like to improve?

2. How would you like your body to feel after practicing somatic techniques?

Step 4: Identify your strengths and resources.

1. What personal strengths (like persistence, curiosity, or creativity) will help you achieve these goals?

2. Who or what can support you in this journey (e.g., friends, family, teachers, or specific resources)?

Step 5: Create a small action plan.

1. What is one small somatic technique you can start practicing today to help you reach your goals?

2. When and where will you practice this technique?

Step 6: Check-In with Yourself

- How will you know you're making progress (e.g., feeling more calm, less tension, better focus)?

By taking the time to reflect and set your goals, you're already taking an important first step toward creating a stronger connection between your mind and body. Keep this worksheet as a reminder of your goals, and revisit it often to see how far you've come!

2

ENHANCING SELF-AWARENESS & EMOTIONAL INTELLIGENCE

"Your emotions are the slaves to your thoughts, and you are the slave to your emotions."

— ELIZABETH GILBERT

Self-awareness might sound fancy, but it's pretty simple and valuable. It means getting to know yourself better by understanding your thoughts, feelings, and the signals your body sends you. Think of it like being your own detective, picking up on the clues your mind, emotions, and body are giving you about how you're doing.

Here's where it gets even cooler: Pairing self-awareness with somatic practices can help you tune into what your body is telling you. Recognizing whether your body feels stressed, relaxed, or somewhere in between can totally change how you handle life's ups and downs.

Imagine you're super nervous about a big game. Without self-awareness, that anxiety might feel like a huge, overwhelming, paralyzing fog. You might end up snapping at your friends or playing terribly. But if you're tuned in, you might notice your sweaty palms, tight chest, and racing thoughts like, "What if I fail?" Once you spot those signs, you can take action and calm yourself down with a quick somatic exercise.

These simple practices teach you how to listen to your body and translate its signals into actions you can take. They're like cheat codes for handling life's challenges in a calmer, more controlled way. And when you approach this with curiosity instead of judgment, you'll feel more grounded no matter what's happening around you.

With self-awareness and somatic techniques in your toolkit, you'll be better equipped to handle anything—from exam stress to everyday ups and downs—while staying calm and in control.

HOW DOES SELF-AWARENESS HELP YOU?

Let's look at how self-awareness helped one teen turn her fear into success:

Sydney, a 17-year-old, came to therapy feeling full of self-doubt. She had big dreams but was too scared to take risks because she feared rejection and failure.

She wanted to put herself out there but couldn't shake the "what ifs" holding her back.

As Sydney started to build self-awareness, she realized how often her negative self-talk stopped her. She'd tell herself things like, "You'll mess it up," or, "Why even bother?" This kept her from chasing amazing opportunities. However, once she noticed this pattern, she began replacing those thoughts with more honest and helpful ones. Through therapy and reflection, she discovered her inner strengths and how much better she felt when focused on them.

Instead of doubting herself, Sydney started thinking, "I can handle this," and, "I'm smart enough to figure things out." This new mindset gave her the courage to try out for the school play, something she'd always wanted to do but was too afraid to risk. She was still nervous, but she used her self-awareness and newly learned emotional intelligence (EI) skills to push through. She gave it her best shot and landed a small role!

Not long after, Sydney burst into her therapy session, grinning ear to ear. "It worked!" she exclaimed. "I used what you taught me to change my negative thoughts, and I got a part!"

Sydney's story shows how powerful self-awareness and emotional regulation can be. Without it, she might have stayed stuck in her self-doubt. But by tuning into her thoughts and choosing to focus on her strengths, she found confidence, joy, and success. It's proof that when you know yourself better, you can achieve more than you ever thought possible.

SELF-AWARENESS THROUGH BODY SIGNALS

Self-awareness requires tuning into your internal world—your thoughts, feelings, and the signals your body sends you every day. It's like learning a secret language —the language of your mind and body. Whether you realize it or not, your body is constantly sending you messages about how you're feeling. Think of it as your internal radar system, always scanning and giving you clues about stress, anxiety, excitement, or sadness.

For example, have you ever felt your heart race before a big test or presentation? That's your body's way of saying, "Hey, I'm nervous!" Or maybe you've noticed a knot in your stomach when something upset you, even if you couldn't quite figure out why. Your emotions and physical sensations are tightly connected, and understanding those signals helps you get a clearer picture of what's happening inside.

By paying attention to these signals, you can learn how to respond in ways that make you feel better. Tight shoulders might mean you've been carrying stress all day and need to stretch or take a break. A racing heart could be a signal to pause and take a few deep breaths to calm down. Feeling jittery? That's your body's way of saying it's time to move—try a quick walk or some stretching to release that energy.

What's cool is that this connection works both ways. Your emotions show up in your body, but by addressing what you feel physically, you can shift how you feel emotionally. Listening to and responding to your body's signals builds a stronger connection with yourself. Over time, it can help you manage your emotions better, clear your mind, and stay in control no matter what life throws your way.

Techniques for Identifying Bodily Signals

Here are two easy techniques to help you tune in:

Bodily Awareness Meditations

This technique involves slowing down, tuning into the present moment, and paying attention to your body and surroundings without judgment. Start by finding a quiet spot where you can sit or lie down comfortably. Close your eyes and take a few deep breaths to relax. Then, focus on your breath—notice if it's fast or slow, shallow or deep. Don't try to change anything; just observe. Does it have a steady rhythm, or does it change depending on how you feel?

As you breathe, begin to scan your body from head to toe. Pay attention to any sensations—tightness, warmth, tingling, or heaviness. For example, you might notice a fluttery feeling in your stomach when you're nervous or tight in your neck after a tough day. You can also tune into your surroundings: What sounds do you hear? How does the air feel on your skin?

These small moments of awareness act like a flashlight, helping you notice emotions or stress signals you might otherwise miss. If you realize your breathing is shallow, you can intentionally slow it down to calm your body. This simple practice helps you connect with how your emotions show up in your body, creating a sense of calm and understanding—no judgment, just awareness.

Signal-Tracking Exercises

Take a moment during the day to pause and ask yourself, "How's my body feeling right now?" Maybe your shoulders feel tight, your palms are a little sweaty, or your heart is racing. No need to overthink it—just notice. To go deeper, try a body scan: Close your eyes and mentally check in with each part of your body, starting from your head and working your way down to your toes. Are your shoulders scrunched up? Is your jaw clenched? Do your legs feel jittery, or is your stomach doing flips?

Grab your phone or a notebook and jot down what you notice. Over time, you might start to see patterns. For example, maybe your chest feels lighter after you do some deep breathing, or you notice your jaw gets tight whenever you're feeling stressed. These clues are like secret messages from your body, helping you figure out what's working and what's not.

Practicing this kind of body awareness is like leveling up your emotional radar. Pretty soon, you'll recognize how your body reacts to stress, anxiety, or other emotions. The more you tune in, the more you'll feel in control when life throws you curveballs. It's like building a cheat sheet for handling tough moments so you can navigate them with confidence and calm.

Why These Practices Matter

Mindful observation and body scans are tools for translating the signals your body sends you. They help you connect your physical sensations with your emotions, making it easier to handle stress and challenges with a sense of calm and control.

By practicing these techniques regularly, you'll start to feel more in tune with yourself. Whether managing difficult emotions or simply understanding what your body needs, self-awareness gives you the power to respond thoughtfully instead of just emotionally reacting. It will allow you to navigate life with confidence and clarity.

INTERPRETING BODY SIGNALS

Your body is like your personal messenger, often giving you hints about your emotions before your brain fully catches up. Learning to understand these signals may feel like learning a new language, but once you do, it's a helpful tool for managing stress and navigating your emotions.

Think about it:

- If your chest feels tight or your breathing gets short, your body might be saying, "Hey, I'm anxious!" This is part of your "fight or flight" response, gearing you up to handle a perceived threat.

- Stiff shoulders or a tense neck? That's often a sign of stress or frustration, especially if you've been carrying a mental load all day.
- Butterflies in your stomach could mean excitement—or maybe nerves. A pit in your stomach, though, might be fear or dread.

Even subtler signs can tell you a lot:

- Heaviness in your arms or legs might mean sadness or emotional exhaustion.
- Clenched fists or a tight jaw could signal anger or frustration bubbling under the surface.
- A tingling sensation in your hands or feet? Depending on the situation, that could mean you're feeling energized—or tense.

The key is to approach these signals with curiosity, not judgment. Instead of thinking, "Why am I feeling this way?" try asking, "What is my body trying to tell me?" It's okay if the answer doesn't come immediately—just recognizing the feeling is the first step toward understanding it.

When you start to decode your body's messages, you can respond intentionally instead of reacting impulsively. For example:

- If you notice tension, try stretching or taking a few deep breaths instead of being short and taking it out on someone.
- If your heart is racing, a grounding practice can help you slow down and feel in control instead of having a panic attack.

The more you practice listening to your body, the better you'll manage emotions with confidence and clarity. You'll have the tools to handle stress and stay in charge of your emotional world.

THE VAGUS NERVE IS YOUR SECRET SUPERPOWER

Ever wonder how some people seem to bounce back from stress like it's no big deal? Their secret might be their vagus nerve at work. The vagus nerve, sometimes called the "wandering nerve," is like a highway connecting your brain to your body. It helps control important things like your heart rate, digestion, and even your ability to calm down when life gets tough.

Think of the vagus nerve as your personal stress-busting superhero. When it's activated, it sends signals to your body that it's safe to relax, shifting you out of "fight or flight" mode and into a state of calm. This is especially important for teens, as juggling school, friendships, and extracurriculars can sometimes feel like walking a tightrope.

Here's the cool part: You can train your vagus nerve to work even better by using somatic practices—simple exercises that connect your mind and body. Things like deep breathing, humming, or even splashing your face with cold water stimulate the vagus nerve, helping you feel calmer and more in control. When your vagus nerve is strong and healthy, it boosts your emotional resilience, making it easier to handle life's ups and downs without feeling totally overwhelmed.

By including vagus nerve activation techniques through somatic therapy in your daily routine, you're managing stress and building a foundation for long-term emotional strength. The next time life throws a curveball, you'll be ready to catch it like a pro.

MASTERING BODY SIGNALS WITH HRV

Have you ever noticed how your body reacts when you're stressed versus when you're calm? Maybe your heart races when you're about to give a presentation or slows down when you're chilling with friends. That's your heart adjusting to what's happening around you. But here's something interesting—your heart doesn't beat like a metronome. There are tiny variations in the timing between each beat, called heart rate variability (HRV), and these little changes say a lot about how your body handles stress.

Think of HRV as your body's resilience meter. A higher HRV means your body can quickly switch gears between stress and relaxation, like a well-tuned car. This makes you better equipped to handle challenges, whether a tough math test or a disagreement with a friend. On the flip side, a lower HRV might signal that your body is stuck in stress mode, struggling to recover. The good news? You can train your body to improve HRV, just like you'd practice shooting hoops or learn a new dance move.

How Does HRV Biofeedback Work?

HRV biofeedback helps you understand your body's reactions in real time. Devices like smartwatches or apps can track your HRV, giving you instant feedback on how your body responds to stress or relaxation techniques. For example, if you're feeling anxious, you might try a deep breathing exercise and watch your HRV improve on the app. It's a reminder that what you do—like breathing deeply or practicing mindfulness—can actually change how your body feels.

Let's say you've got a big exam coming up, and your HRV shows that you're stressed (low HRV). You can take a moment to breathe slowly or stretch, and you might see your HRV rise. This feedback helps you connect the dots between your actions and your emotions, making it easier to manage stress and feel more in control.

Why Does HRV Matter?

HRV isn't just about stress—it's about the connection between your body and emotions. By tracking and improving your HRV, you can spot stress signals early, like a racing heart or tight muscles, and take steps to calm yourself before things spiral. Over time, practicing HRV biofeedback trains your nervous system to bounce back from stress faster, helping you feel steadier no matter what life throws at you.

Whether you're managing school pressure, navigating social challenges, or just dealing with the ups and downs of being a teen, HRV biofeedback gives you tools to stay calm and confident.

Understanding HRV and its connection to your body's signals is about thriving through stressful moments. By learning to listen to your body and using tools like HRV biofeedback, you're building skills to help you feel more in charge of your emotions and more connected to yourself.

CULTIVATING SELF-COMPASSION

Being kind to yourself can be challenging, but self-compassion can significantly improve mental health. You're not alone if you often criticize your thoughts, judge yourself harshly, are paralyzed by perfectionism, or blame yourself for small mistakes. Negative self-talk comes naturally to many, but it can harm your self-worth. Self-compassion involves treating yourself with the same kindness and understanding you'd offer a friend, especially when you make mistakes. Everyone struggles, and you can learn to show yourself patience instead of judgment.

The way you talk to yourself impacts every part of your life. Harsh self-criticism increases anxiety, sadness, and insecurity, while self-compassion boosts confidence, motivation, and resilience. Research shows that practicing self-compassion not only lowers the risk of mental health challenges but also helps you bounce back more quickly from life's difficulties.

How Somatic Therapy Fosters Self-Compassion

Somatic therapy strengthens self-compassion by encouraging mindfulness, self-awareness, and self-acceptance. It emphasizes that your body holds valuable information about your emotions and experiences. Tuning into your body's cues without judgment can help you develop a more compassionate relationship with yourself.

Somatic practices such as body scans and mindful breathing encourage you to reflect on physical sensations, like tightness in your chest or tension in your shoulders, and ask yourself, "What might this be trying to tell me?" This approach helps you connect with your emotions without criticism or impatience, fostering kindness toward yourself.

Somatic therapy also helps you recognize that your body's reactions—like feeling stressed, nervous, or upset—are natural responses to life's challenges. Instead of becoming frustrated with yourself, you can use somatic techniques like deep breathing or gentle stretches to calm your body. These practices signal your nervous system to relax, allowing you to approach your emotions with understanding and patience.

For teens who struggle with body image or feel disconnected from their physical selves, somatic therapy offers a way to reconnect in a positive, accepting way. By paying attention to your body without judgment, you can learn to appreciate its strengths, resilience, and ability to communicate with you.

Exercises to Develop Self-Compassion

Self-Kindness Meditation

Find a quiet space where you can sit comfortably. Close your eyes and take a few deep breaths. Notice any areas of tension in your body and, instead of trying to fix them, focus on treating them with kindness. Imagine sending warmth and care to those areas while repeating phrases like, "It's okay to feel this way" or "I'm doing my best." This simple practice helps replace self-criticism with self-compassion.

Criticism-Reduction Practice

When you catch yourself thinking negatively, pause and check in with your body. Notice any areas of stress or discomfort. Take a deep breath, imagining yourself exhaling tension and inhaling compassion. Repeat affirmations like, "I am enough just as I am." This helps shift your mindset from negativity to self-kindness.

ENHANCING SELF-ESTEEM AND BODY IMAGE

Self-esteem and body image are deeply connected to how you view and interact with your physical and emotional self. Self-esteem is your sense of self-worth, while body image is how you feel about your physical appearance. For many teens, body image challenges are shaped by comparisons, social media, and cultural pressures. Somatic therapy provides tools to rebuild a loving and accepting relationship with your body, helping to boost both self-esteem and body image.

Somatic techniques like body scans, grounding exercises, and mindful movement help you focus less on appearance and more on how your body feels and functions. For example, noticing the strength in your legs as you walk or the calmness that comes from a deep breath helps you appreciate your body for what it does, not just how it looks.

Developing self-esteem through somatic therapy also involves reducing self-criticism and embracing self-compassion. Accepting and valuing your body without judgment creates a foundation for improved mental health, stronger resilience, and a positive self-image.

HOW SOMATIC THERAPY INFLUENCES SELF-PERCEPTION

Somatic therapy shifts your focus from external judgment to internal awareness, promoting a healthier self-perception. You learn to observe your body's signals without criticism through body scans, mindful breathing, and gentle movement. This process helps break the cycle of negative self-talk and self-judgment, encouraging you to appreciate your body for its strength and resilience.

Instead of fixating on perceived flaws, somatic therapy teaches you to value your body for what it can do. Focusing on sensations like the ease of a deep breath or the grounding strength of your legs helps you develop a more accepting and loving attitude toward yourself. Over time, this perspective enhances your self-esteem and body image, making you feel more confident and secure in your skin.

Exercises to Boost Self-Esteem

Body Positivity Practice

Stand in front of a mirror and focus on the parts of your body you appreciate. This might be your smile, strong legs, or relaxed posture. Place your hands on the area you value and take a few deep breaths, thanking your body for everything it does. Replace negative thoughts with affirmations like, "My body is strong and capable" or "I appreciate the way my body supports me."

Confidence-Building Movements

Try a power pose to feel more grounded and in control. Stand tall with your feet shoulder-width apart, shoulders back, chest lifted, and arms at your sides or spread wide. Hold this pose while taking deep breaths for two minutes. Imagine yourself radiating strength and confidence. This simple exercise helps boost your self-assurance and shift your self-image toward positivity.

EMOTIONAL INTELLIGENCE WITH SOMATIC AWARENESS

Emotional intelligence (EI) is the ability to recognize, understand, and manage your own emotions while also being able to understand and influence the emotions of others. It's about realizing how emotions shape behavior—for better or worse—and using that knowledge to improve how you react to situations and connect with others.

Psychologist Daniel Goleman developed a popular model of EI, breaking it down into five main components (Lea 2023):

1. **Self-Awareness**: Self-awareness is about understanding your emotions and being able to express them clearly. It means recognizing how you feel, why you feel that way, and how those emotions can impact your actions.

2. **Self-Regulation**: Once you're aware of your emotions, self-regulation helps you manage them. It requires pausing instead of reacting impulsively when a strong emotion hits. For example, if you feel

frustration building, self-regulation helps you step back, take a deep breath, and choose how to respond instead of lashing out.

3. **Motivation**: Motivation is the drive to work toward your goals, even when things get tough. High EI helps you stay focused and push through challenges by keeping your eyes on the long-term benefits instead of getting discouraged.

4. **Empathy**: Empathy refers to understanding and being sensitive to the emotions of others. It means picking up on subtle cues in someone's facial expressions, tone of voice, or body language to get a clearer sense of their feelings.

5. **Social Skills**: Strong EI improves your ability to connect with others, communicate effectively, and build relationships. It's what helps you maintain friendships and work through conflicts with understanding and respect.

How Does Somatic Therapy Improve EI?

Somatic therapy enhances emotional intelligence by strengthening the connection between your body and emotions. Your body constantly sends signals—like tension, restlessness, or warmth—that reflect how you're feeling. Learning to tune into these physical cues helps you understand your emotions more clearly and take control of how you respond.

For example, a tight chest might signal anxiety, while heavy limbs could mean sadness. By noticing these sensations, somatic therapy helps you link your physical experiences to your emotions, giving you a clearer understanding of what you're feeling and why. This heightened body awareness naturally leads to better self-regulation.

When you know how your body reacts to different emotions, you can use somatic techniques like grounding, deep breathing, or mindful movement to calm your body and regain control. Over time, these strategies become second nature, helping you handle challenges with confidence and balance.

Somatic therapy also boosts empathy. When you understand how emotions feel in your own body—like the racing heart of anxiety or the furrowed brow of anger —it's easier to recognize similar signs in others. This deeper awareness helps you connect with people on a more genuine level, respond with understanding, and build stronger relationships.

Somatic therapy helps sharpen emotional intelligence by combining body awareness and emotional understanding. It gives you the tools to stay calm under pressure, connect with others more deeply, and approach life's challenges more confidently and clearly.

Somatic Exercises for Emotional Mastery

Somatic therapy offers practical exercises that can help you develop emotional regulation and emotional intelligence (EI). These techniques not only help you better control your own emotions but also make it easier to connect with others.

Alternate Nostril Breathing: A Simple Tool for Calm

When life feels overwhelming, alternate nostril breathing can help you find balance and calm. This technique, rooted in yoga, is all about breathing through one nostril at a time to relax your body, sharpen your focus, and boost your emotional resilience. It's like giving your brain a reset button while keeping your energy steady and centered.

Here's how it works: Start by sitting comfortably with your back straight. Close your right nostril with your thumb and inhale deeply through your left nostril. Then, close your left nostril with your ring finger, release your right nostril, and exhale fully through the right side. Switch sides and repeat for a few cycles—or as long as it feels good.

This simple practice reduces stress, improves focus, and helps you stay in the moment. Plus, it's easy to do anywhere—whether you're prepping for a test or just need a quick breather from a busy day. Give it a try and feel the difference!

Progressive Muscle Relaxation (PMR)

PMR is a great way to reduce emotional reactivity by helping you identify and release physical tension, which is often linked to stress, anxiety, and trauma. In this exercise, you tense and relax different muscle groups one at a time, starting with your toes and working up to your head. For example, you might tense your feet for a few seconds, hold the tension, then slowly release it. This teaches you to notice the difference between tension and relaxation, helping you recognize when your body is stressed and giving you tools to calm down. PMR doesn't just relax your muscles—it also soothes your nervous system, leaving you feeling emotionally balanced.

Tension Release Techniques

These techniques are designed to help your body let go of built-up tension caused by intense emotions. Simple movements like shaking out your arms or gently swaying from side to side can work wonders for releasing pent-up energy. By physically processing emotional stress, these exercises can help you feel clearer and calmer. Regularly practicing tension release teaches you to manage emotional outbursts before they escalate while helping you become more in tune with your body.

Emotion Identification Activities

Identifying and labeling your emotions is a key part of emotional intelligence. With somatic therapy, you can practice this by taking a few minutes to close your eyes, take deep breaths, and scan your body for sensations. Pay attention to what you feel—a tight chest might signal sadness, while a fluttery stomach could indicate nervousness. You can respond thoughtfully rather than impulsively once you connect these sensations to specific emotions. Over time, this practice strengthens your ability to understand your emotions and how they show up in your body.

Empathy-Building Practices

One simple exercise to help you connect with others is "embodied listening," where you focus on a conversation while noticing your physical reactions. For example, if someone shares something upsetting, you might feel a tightness in your chest. Recognizing these responses helps you respond with genuine empathy. Another technique is subtly mirroring the other person's body language, creating a stronger emotional connection and improving mutual understanding. These practices enhance your ability to empathize and build more supportive, meaningful relationships.

Somatic therapy gives you practical, hands-on ways to develop emotional intelligence. Whether you're calming yourself with PMR, identifying emotions through body awareness, or connecting with others through empathy-building exercises, these techniques help you navigate emotions with confidence and care.

Download your interactive chapter worksheets _NOW_ to apply these techniques, track your progress, and build real emotional resilience—one step at a time.

SCAN QR CODE FOR DOWNLOADABLE WORKSHEETS

INTERACTIVE WORKSHEET

Here are some practical interactive worksheet ideas to help you track your progress, reflect on somatic exercises, and build emotional resilience for your emotional toolbox.

Worksheet 1: Daily Emotional Check-In

Purpose: To help you track your emotional states and recognize patterns in your feelings and responses.

Instructions: Every day, take a moment to reflect on your emotional state. Use this worksheet to identify how you're feeling and which tools you used to manage your emotions. This will help you notice which somatic practices work best for you.

Emotional Check-In:

1. Date: _____Beginning HRV: _____
2. How are you feeling right now? (Check all that apply)
   - Happy
   - Anxious
   - Angry

- ○ Sad
- ○ Overwhelmed
- ○ Stressed
- ○ Calm
- ○ Other: _____

3. What physical sensations are you noticing in your body?
    - ○ Tightness in the chest
    - ○ Tension in shoulders
    - ○ Racing heartbeat
    - ○ Stomach discomfort
    - ○ Heavy or light feeling in limbs
    - ○ Other: _____

4. Which somatic tool(s) did you use today?
    - ○ Grounding techniques (e.g., feet on the floor)
    - ○ Deep breathing exercises (e.g., belly breathing, box breathing)
    - ○ Movement (e.g., stretching, walking)
    - ○ Meditation or mindfulness practices
    - ○ Journaling
    - ○ Other: _____

5. How did these tools help you feel? (Rate 1-5: 1 being not helpful, five being very helpful)
    - ○ Grounding: ____
    - ○ Breathing: ____
    - ○ Movement: ____
    - ○ Other tools: ____

6. What would you do differently next time? (Optional reflection)

_____

7. What progress have you noticed in your emotional regulation?

- ◦ More aware of my emotions
- ◦ More calm in stressful situations
- ◦ Better able to recognize physical cues in my body
- ◦ Other: _____
8. Ending HRV: _____

Worksheet 2: Somatic Exercise Reflection

Purpose: To help you reflect on the somatic exercises you've practiced and how they impact your emotions and physical state.

Instructions: Reflect on your experience using the questions below after completing a somatic exercise. This will help you gauge how the exercise affects you and which techniques work best.

Somatic Exercise Reflection:

1. Exercise completed: (e.g., body scan, progressive muscle relaxation, breathing exercise)

   _____

2. When did you practice the exercise?
   - ◦ Morning
   - ◦ Afternoon
   - ◦ Evening
3. What were you feeling before doing the exercise? (Check all that apply)
   - ◦ Anxious
   - ◦ Angry
   - ◦ Stressed
   - ◦ Sad
   - ◦ Calm
   - ◦ Other: _____

4. What sensations did you notice in your body before the exercise?
   - Tension
   - Racing heartbeat
   - Shallow breathing
   - Restlessness
   - Other: _____

5. Describe your experience during the exercise:

_____

6. What physical sensations or emotional shifts did you notice after the exercise?

_____

7. How did your mood change after completing the exercise?
   - More relaxed
   - More energized
   - Less anxious
   - Other: _____

8. How did your HRV respond to the exercise?
   _____

9. How likely are you to use this exercise again? (Rate 1-5: 1 being not likely, five being very likely)

_____

10. Any additional thoughts or observations?

_____

3

PRACTICAL EXERCISES FOR STRESS & ANXIETY

"Anxiety does not empty tomorrow of its sorrows, but only empties today of its strength."

— CHARLES SPURGEON

Teens who are good at handling stress and anxiety stay healthy! Imagine it as if you were tightening the guitar strings. When the strings are plucked without tension, they produce an odd sound. Overtightening them will cause the strings to break. Making good music requires figuring out how much tension to put on the strings. Similarly, it's critical to learn how to manage stress and anxiety so the body can adapt to the amount of tension it can tolerate. Incorporating relaxation techniques and physical activity into our daily routines is a great way to attain balance.

QUICK STRESS BUSTERS FOR BUSY TEENS

Let's face it—life can get hectic. Finding time to deal with stress might be impossible between classes, extracurriculars, and just trying to stay sane. That's where quick and easy exercises come in. These are like your mental "snacks" for when life gets over-whelming. The best part? They only take a minute or two and can be done anytime, anywhere—whether you're at school, hanging out with friends, or even chilling at home. Here are three go-to techniques that can help you reset your mood and vibe quickly.

30-Second Breathing Reset

Think of this as a "Ctrl+Alt+Delete" for your brain. Here's how:

- Sit or stand comfortably and take a deep breath through your nose for a count of four.
- Hold your breath for four counts.
- Slowly exhale through your mouth for six counts.
- Repeat this for 30 seconds, focusing on the feeling of your breath moving in and out.

It's quick, calming, and can help you feel more in control—perfect for those moments before a test or after a stressful convo.

Finger Tapping Exercise

This one's sneaky (in a good way) because no one will even know you're doing it. It helps distract your mind and brings you back to the present.

- Touch the tip of your thumb to the tip of your index finger and say to yourself, "I'm calm."
- Move to your middle finger and say, "I'm okay."
- Move to your ring finger and say, "I'm in control."
- End with your pinky and say, "I've got this."
- Repeat, on the other hand, if you want.

You can do this while waiting for class, standing in line, or just about anywhere. It's like a mini pep talk you can give yourself any time.

Instant Visualization Techniques

This one's great if you've got a wild imagination. Close your eyes (or keep them open if you're somewhere public) and picture a peaceful scene, like a beach or a cozy forest.

- Imagine the sights, sounds, and smells around you—waves crashing, birds chirping, the salty breeze.
- Take a few deep breaths while you stay in that mental space.
- Open your eyes and bring that calm feeling back into the real world.

It's like a mini vacation for your brain. The best thing about these stress busters? They're portable and low key. You can do them in a busy hallway or at your desk without drawing attention. Plus, when you make them a habit, they add up. Think of them like tiny building blocks for your emotional health—each time you do one, you're making it easier for your brain and body to handle stress next time.

THE ROLE OF MINDFULNESS IN SOMATIC THERAPY

Let's talk mindfulness. You've probably heard the word before—maybe in a yoga class, a meditation app, or someone saying, "Just be mindful!" But what does it mean, especially when it comes to somatic therapy? Mindfulness is all about staying connected to the now. It means paying attention to what's happening now —your thoughts, emotions, and body sensations—without letting your brain wander off into overthinking or worry-town. In somatic therapy, mindfulness takes this further by helping you focus on how your body feels and moves, making every exercise more effective.

Think about it this way: You're scrolling through social media, your brain bounces between five different thoughts, and you barely even notice how your body feels. Sound familiar? Mindfulness flips the script. You're grounding yourself in the present by tuning into your body—how your feet feel on the floor, how your chest rises and falls with each breath. This "present-moment focus" is key in somatic therapy because it helps you notice and respond to what your body is trying to tell you.

When you practice "mindful body awareness," you're training yourself to recognize physical sensations like tension, calmness, or stress signals. The more you do this, the better you understand how your emotions show up in your body and what you can do to feel better.

Mindful Breathing and Movement Exercises

Mindfulness isn't just sitting cross-legged and chanting "om." Here are two real-life ways to bring mindfulness into your life with somatic therapy.

Mindful Walking:

Next time you're walking (to class, to the fridge, or wherever), try this:

- Focus on the sensation of your feet touching the ground.
- Notice the rhythm of your steps and how your arms swing naturally.
- Tune into what's around you—the sounds, smells, and sights.

It turns an ordinary walk into a calming mini adventure.

Breathing with Awareness:

This one's a lifesaver for stressful moments.

- Sit or stand comfortably and close your eyes if you can.
- Inhale deeply through your nose and pay attention to how the air feels going into your lungs.
- Exhale slowly through your mouth and feel the tension leaving your body.
- Do this for a minute or two while focusing only on your breath.

These small, mindful actions can help you chill out fast and reset your vibe. Here's the science part: Mindfulness has been shown to reduce anxiety and help people feel more emotionally stable. Slowing down and focusing gives your brain a break from all the chaos. It's like hitting pause on stress to feel more in control. And when you make mindfulness a habit, it can seriously boost your mental health game over time.

How to Make Mindfulness a Daily Thing

You don't need a yoga mat or hours of free time to be mindful—it's something you can slip into your daily life without even breaking a sweat.

- **Mindfulness in Daily Tasks:** Try being fully present during stuff you already do, like brushing your teeth or eating a snack. Pay attention to the taste, texture, or even the sound of what you're doing. It might sound small, but it makes a big difference in training your mind to focus.
- **Mindful Moments:** Set aside just one minute a day to stop and check in with yourself. It could be right before bed, during lunch, while commuting, or even during a busy day. Use that time to breathe, stretch, or notice how your body feels.

Mindfulness doesn't mean being perfect or zen all the time—it proclaims that you are showing up for yourself in small but mighty ways. By adding these techniques to your emotional toolbox, you're setting yourself up to handle stress, build resilience, and feel more connected to your body and mind.

VAGUS NERVE ACTIVATION FOR MANAGING STRESS

We briefly mentioned the vagus nerve in the previous chapter. You might not know much about it yet. This hidden superstar in your body dramatically impacts how you handle stress, emotions, and even trauma. Understanding and working with your vagus nerve can help you feel more grounded, calm, and controlled.

The vagus nerve is like a highway that connects your brain to major parts of your body, including your heart, lungs, and digestive system. Think of it as the communication system that helps your body chill out after stress. When you've been through trauma, your vagus nerve might not work as smoothly as it should, leaving you feeling stuck in fight-or-flight mode—basically, always on edge. Activating the vagus nerve can help signal your body that it's safe to relax, which is a big deal for trauma recovery.

Ready to take control of your stress and trauma symptoms? Here are some easy, low-key exercises that can wake up your vagus nerve and help you feel more balanced:

Humming Your Favorite Tune

Did you know that humming can help you relax? The vibrations from humming stimulate the vagus nerve, signaling to your body that it's okay to chill out. Pick a song you love or something soothing like "Om." Take a deep breath in through your nose and, as you exhale, hum softly, feeling the vibrations in your throat and chest. Repeat this for a few minutes and notice how your body starts to feel calmer and more grounded.

Deep Breathing With a Twist

Your breath acts like a remote control for your nervous system, and a little tweak can make it even more effective. Sit comfortably and take a deep breath in through your nose for four seconds. Hold your breath for another four seconds, then exhale slowly through your mouth for six seconds. The key to activating your vagus nerve is a long, steady exhale, so focus on making it slow and controlled.

Splash of Cool Calm

A little cold water can work wonders for calming both your body and mind. Splash your face with cold water when you're feeling stressed or overwhelmed, and focus on the refreshing sensation. For an extra boost, place a cool washcloth on the back of your neck or chest. This simple technique can quickly bring your attention back to the present moment while helping your body relax.

Gentle Neck Massage

The vagus nerve is close to the surface in certain spots, like your neck, making it an easy target for activation. Use your fingertips to gently massage the sides of your neck, just below your jawline. Apply light pressure and make small circular motions. Not only does this activate the vagus nerve, but it also feels incredibly soothing.

Belly Breathing

Also known as diaphragmatic breathing, this exercise helps activate your vagus nerve while grounding you. Sit or lie down in a comfortable spot and place one hand on your chest and the other on your belly. Breathe deeply into your belly, letting it rise like a balloon while keeping your chest still. Exhale fully and let your belly fall. This simple technique can calm your nervous system and leave you feeling more balanced.

These quick and easy exercises are like little resets for your nervous system, helping you feel more balanced and ready to take on whatever comes your way. Try them out and see which ones work best for you!

Physiological Benefits of Vagus Nerve Activation

Why does all this matter? Activating your vagus nerve has some amazing effects on your body and emotions.

One big benefit is improved heart rate variability (HRV), a fancy way of saying your body gets better at adapting to stress. A healthy HRV means you're more resilient to tough situations and can bounce back quicker.

When your vagus nerve is activated, your brain gets signals that help you manage emotions better. Instead of feeling overwhelmed, you can experience more balance and calm, even during stressful times.

The great thing about these exercises is that they're quick, simple, and can be done anywhere. Try adding these exercises to your morning or bedtime routine. For example, start your day with a few deep breaths or end it with a humming session to wind down.

You can also combine vagus nerve exercises with your other self-care habits. For example, you could hum while you stretch or massage your neck during a study break. These small moments can make a big difference in how you feel throughout the day.

By taking care of your vagus nerve, you're giving yourself a powerful tool to handle stress, recover from trauma, and feel more in control of your emotions. It's all about creating space for healing, one small step at a time.

STRETCHING EXERCISES FOR ANXIETY RELIEF

Ever notice how your shoulders creep up toward your ears or your neck feels tight when stressed? That's your body holding onto tension, and it can make anxiety even worse. Physical tension and anxiety are like partners in crime—when one shows up, the other often tags along. But here's the good news: Stretching can help break up this duo. Stretching loosens up those tight muscles and signals to your brain that it's okay to relax.

Let's discuss some easy stretches to help you chill out and feel more comfortable.

Neck and Shoulder Release Stretches

Start by tilting your head gently to one side, bringing your ear toward your shoulder. Hold for a few breaths, then switch sides. You can also roll your shoulders forward and backward in slow, smooth circles. These moves help release tension when hunched over your phone or backpack.

Spinal Relaxation Sequences

Sit cross-legged or on a chair, gently twist your torso to one side, placing a hand on your knee for support. Hold for a few breaths, then switch. Or try a simple forward fold, letting your head hang and breathing deeply as you feel your spine stretch out. It's like hitting the reset button for your back after a long day.

Leg and Hip Tension Relief

For your legs, stretch one out straight before you while keeping the other foot tucked in. Reach for your toes or as far as you comfortably can. For your hips, try a butterfly stretch—sit down, bring the soles of your feet together, and let your knees gently fall outward. These stretches feel amazing after sitting for too long.

Don't worry if you're not super flexible—stretching is for everyone. If a stretch feels too intense, ease off or try a modified version, like bending your knees in a forward fold instead of keeping them straight. Always pay attention to your posture and avoid bouncing; slow and steady is the way to go.

Think of stretching as your daily chill pill. It only takes a few minutes, but the benefits stack up over time. Try adding stretches to your morning routine to start the day relaxed or doing a few before bed to wind down. Even just a quick stretch break during school can make a huge difference to keep anxiety in check.

Stretching isn't just about flexibility—it's about feeling good in your body and giving your mind some much-needed peace.

TECHNIQUES TO OVERCOME BURNOUT

Let's take a deep dive into burnout—a state of exhaustion that can leave you stuck in slow motion, no matter how much sleep or rest you get. It's not just about being tired after a busy day; it's a more serious state of emotional, mental, and physical depletion. For teens, burnout often sneaks up when you're trying to juggle everything at once—school, sports, social life, family expectations, and maybe even a part-time job. The signs can vary: You might feel constantly overwhelmed, irritable, and unable to concentrate. Maybe you feel like everything is too much or that you have to drag yourself through each day without motivation. On the physical side, burnout can be headaches, body aches, trouble sleeping, or even frequent colds because your body is under so much stress.

Here's the kicker: Burnout affects more than just your energy levels. It also affects your mood, your relationships, and even your sense of purpose. Ignoring the problem can make it worse, so recognizing burnout early is your first step toward reclaiming your balance.

Somatic Strategies to Combat Burnout

One of the best ways to tackle burnout is to reconnect with your body through somatic practices.

Restorative yoga is an awesome place to start. This isn't your high-intensity yoga class; it's more like "relax and let go" yoga. Imagine lying on your back with your legs stretched up against a wall. Sounds easy, right? It is—but this simple pose can work magic by reducing tension in your lower back, returning blood flow to your brain, and helping you feel grounded.

Breathwork is another good strategy. When your stress levels are through the roof, your breathing tends to get shallow and fast, making things worse. Taking control of your breath can help you reset. Try box breathing: Inhale deeply for four counts, hold your breath for another four, and then exhale for four counts. Repeat this for a few minutes, and you'll feel your body relax. It's like hitting the refresh button on your mind.

The Power of Self-Care and Balance

Maybe you've heard this before, and it's true: You can't pour from an empty cup. Burnout happens when you keep giving 100% to everything around you without refilling your energy tank. This is why self-care isn't a luxury—it's a necessity. And no, self-care isn't just bubble baths and spa days (although those are great, too!). It could be blasting your favorite playlist, drawing, playing basketball, or even zoning out with a video game—whatever makes you feel good. The key is to prioritize time for these activities, no matter how busy you are.

Self-care also means knowing when to hit the brakes. If your schedule is packed with back-to-back obligations, ask yourself, "What can I cut out?" Learning to say no to things that don't serve you is one of the most powerful ways to protect your energy.

Managing Workload and Stress Effectively

Preventing burnout isn't just about fixing it once it happens—it's about staying ahead of it. Start by getting a handle on your time. Use a planner or a scheduling app like Microsoft To-Do (https://to-do.office.com/tasks/), Google Calendar (https://calendar.google.com), or My Study Life (https://mystudylife.com/) to manage your schedule and block out chunks of your day for studying, relaxing, and recharging. When you see everything mapped out, balancing your priorities is easier.

Set realistic goals, too. You don't need to ace every test, win every game, and be there for every friend simultaneously. Perfection isn't the goal—balance is. And if things get overwhelming, talk to someone. Whether it's your parent or guardian, a trusted teacher, a counselor, or a best friend, sharing your stress can make it feel more manageable.

Burnout can feel like an uphill battle, but with the right tools, you can overcome it and build habits that protect your energy in the long run. By making self-care, time management, and somatic practices part of your daily routine, you'll not only bounce back from burnout but also grow stronger, more resilient, and more in tune with yourself.

BALANCING SCHOOL LIFE AND SOMATIC PRACTICES

We know that school can feel like an endless to-do list, and balancing all that pressure while caring for yourself isn't easy. Between assignments, exams, and keeping up with grades, it can feel like there's no time to breathe. In addition, the constant pressure to perform, whether from your expectations or others', might make self-care the last thing on your mind. But if you don't make time for yourself, your brain and body will eventually hit a wall—and that's not good for anyone.

Self-care doesn't mean ignoring your responsibilities; it means finding a balance so you can handle them better. Instead of seeing self-care as a distraction, think of it as fuel. Taking short breaks, eating right, and getting enough sleep are all ways to recharge so you can show up stronger for school.

Athlete Pressures and the Need for Self-Care

If you're an athlete, you know the drill: practice, games, conditioning, and somehow fitting in schoolwork in between. Being part of a team can be amazing, but it also comes with high expectations—always performing your best, staying in peak condition, and never letting the team down. The physical demands are intense, and without proper self-care, it's easy to burn out or get injured.

This is why recovery is just as important as training. Stretching, resting, and fueling your body with good nutrition are non-negotiables. And don't underestimate the power of mental recovery—whether that's a guided meditation, deep breathing, or even just zoning out to music for 10 minutes. Prioritizing your mind and body will help you perform better on the field and in the classroom.

Extracurricular Activities and Overcommitment

Maybe you're not an athlete, but your calendar is still packed with clubs, volunteering, music lessons, or part-time work. While extracurriculars are great for building skills and hanging out with friends, overloading yourself can lead to exhaustion. When you say "yes" to everything, you quickly forget to say "yes" to yourself.

The solution? Be intentional about how you spend your time. Instead of trying to do everything, focus on the activities that genuinely make you happy or help you grow. And remember, it's okay to step back from something if it's adding too much stress. Protecting your energy isn't selfish—it's smart.

Integrating Somatic Exercises Into School Life

Somatic practices are designed to fit into your day, helping you stay calm, focused, and ready for whatever comes next.

Here's how you can make them work for you:

Mindful Breaks During Study Sessions

Ever feel like your brain is about to explode after cramming for a test or tackling a big project? That's your cue to hit pause—literally. Taking 2–3 minutes to reset with a mindful break can work wonders for your focus and energy. Try this: Close your eyes, take a deep breath, and let it out slowly. Then, focus on the feeling of your feet touching the ground or the weight of your body in your chair. This simple exercise can clear mental clutter and help you dive back into your work feeling refreshed.

Another option? Set a timer every 30–45 minutes, or use the stand-up reminder on your smartwatch during study sessions to step away. Stretch your arms, roll your shoulders, or stand up and shake it out. These mini movement breaks keep your body from getting stiff and your mind from feeling overwhelmed.

Quick Grounding Exercises Between Classes

It's easy to carry stress from class to class. Grounding exercises are a super-easy way to hit reset between periods. Here's one to try: As you walk to your next class, pay close attention to each step you take. Notice how your feet feel as they hit the ground, the rhythm of your pace, or even the sound of your shoes. It's like a walking meditation—and no one will even know you're doing it.

Another quick trick is the 5-4-3-2-1 grounding exercise when you feel particularly frazzled. Look around and identify five things you can see, four things you can feel, three things you can hear, two things you can smell, and one thing you can taste (or imagine tasting). It only takes a minute and helps bring your focus back to the present.

Somatic Practices in Extracurriculars

Extracurricular activities can be super rewarding, but they also come with their fair share of stress—gearing up for a big game, nailing your performance on stage, or leading a club meeting. The pressure to perform at your best can sometimes feel overwhelming. That's where somatic practices come in! These techniques help you manage stress, boost focus, and control your body and mind to crush it in any activity.

Diaphragmatic Breathing for Calm and Focus

Diaphragmatic breathing is your go-to when nervous before a game, performance, or presentation. This deep breathing technique slows your heart rate, calms your nerves, and helps you focus. Here's how to do it:

- Place one hand on your chest and the other on your stomach.
- Breathe deeply through your nose for about four seconds, letting your stomach rise (not your chest).
- Exhale slowly through your mouth for six seconds, feeling your stomach lower.
- Repeat for a minute or two to feel more grounded and ready to perform.

Progressive Muscle Relaxation (PMR) for Tension Relief

Physical tension often sneaks up when you're stressed. PMR is a great way to release that tension and get into a more relaxed state. Before or after your activity, try this:

- Sit or lie down in a quiet space.
- Start with your feet—tense the muscles for five seconds, then release.
- Work your way up your body, tightening and relaxing different muscle groups (legs, hands, shoulders, etc.).

By the end, you'll feel looser and more at ease, whether prepping to compete or winding down afterward.

Body Scan for Awareness

Staying in tune with your body is essential for performing at your best. A quick body scan helps you assess your feelings and pinpoint areas of tension or discomfort.

- Close your eyes and focus on your breathing.
- Start at your head and slowly move your attention down your body, noticing any tightness or unease.
- If you find tension, breathe into that area and imagine it softening as you exhale.

This practice is perfect for catching and addressing stress signals early before they become overwhelming.

Grounding Techniques for Staying Centered

If you're feeling scattered or overwhelmed during a high-pressure moment, grounding techniques can bring you back to the present. The 5-4-3-2-1 method is especially helpful:

- Look around and identify five things you can see.
- Notice four things you can touch.
- Listen for three things you can hear.
- Smell two things (or imagine scents you like).
- Taste one thing (or think about your favorite snack).

This exercise helps you stay calm and focused no matter the situation.

Visualization for Confidence and Success

Mental rehearsals can boost confidence and reduce anxiety. Visualization involves imagining yourself performing successfully—scoring the winning goal, hitting the perfect note, or acing a debate.

- Close your eyes and picture the scene.
- Imagine every detail: the environment, your movements, and the feeling of accomplishment.
- Repeat this often to build confidence and reduce pre-performance nerves.

Shaking and Movement Release for Pre-Performance Jitters

If your nerves feel like they're about to take over, try shaking them out—literally. Lightly shake your arms, legs, and torso to release pent-up energy. Pair this with gentle stretches to loosen up and feel more grounded before stepping into the spotlight.

TIME MANAGEMENT FOR LIFE BALANCE

Balancing school, activities, and self-care might feel like juggling a million things simultaneously, but good time management can make everything much more manageable. When you're constantly racing against the clock to meet deadlines, finish assignments, or squeeze in practice time, it's easy for self-care to fall to the bottom of your priority list. That's why creating a balanced daily schedule is so important—it gives you the structure to handle your responsibilities and take care of yourself without feeling like you're drowning in stress.

Start by mapping out your day. Write down or add to your scheduling app what you must do—classes, homework, practices, or other commitments. Then, carve out specific times for self-care, like a 10-minute break to stretch, journal, or breathe between study sessions. Don't forget to include downtime to do something you genuinely enjoy, whether gaming, reading, or catching up with friends. Even small pockets of time for yourself can add up and refresh you.

Pro tip: Learn to say no when your schedule gets too packed. Overcommitting is one of the fastest routes to burnout. If your mental health needs attention, it's okay to drop an activity or ask for an extension on an assignment. Managing your time effectively means being honest about what you can handle and prioritizing what truly matters.

TALKING TO PARENTS & TEACHERS ABOUT MENTAL HEALTH

Parents, guardians, teachers, coaches, and school counselors aren't just there to grade your work or guide your performance—they're also your support system. Talking to them about your mental health might feel a little intimidating at first, but it's a crucial step toward getting the help you need.

Coaches can play a unique role in your life. They often see how you handle pressure, teamwork, and challenges in extracurricular activities. Letting them know if you're feeling anxious or overwhelmed can help them understand why you might need a breather or extra encouragement. For example, you could say, "I've been really stressed with school lately, and it's making practices feel harder. Is there a way to adjust my schedule temporarily?" Most coaches value open communication and will appreciate your honesty.

Similarly, parents and guardians can be great allies in helping you navigate mental health challenges. Share your feelings with them, even if it's just a little at a time. Saying something like, "I've been feeling really stressed, and I think I need some help managing everything," can start the conversation. They can advocate for you with teachers or counselors or help you figure out a plan to feel more balanced.

It might not feel very comforting to talk about your mental health, but starting the conversation doesn't have to be a big deal. Try something simple, like emailing your teacher to say, "I've been feeling really overwhelmed lately, and it's affecting my work. Can we talk about how I can stay on track?" Most educators want to help you succeed.

Your school counselor is an excellent resource if you're unsure where to start. They're trained to help with stress, anxiety, and even time management strategies. Whether figuring out how to balance a heavy workload or just having someone to listen, counselors are there to help.

By being open with the adults in your life—whether they're your parents, coaches, or teachers—you're building a network of support that can help you feel more capable and confident, both in and out of the classroom.

Download your interactive chapter worksheets *NOW* to apply these techniques, track your progress, and build real emotional resilience—one step at a time.

SCAN QR CODE FOR DOWNLOADABLE WORKSHEETS

INTERACTIVE WORKSHEET

Section 1: Daily Somatic Exercise Log

Date	Exercise Performed	Duration (Minutes)	How I Felt Before (1-10) *	How I Felt After (1-10) *	Starting HRV	Ending HRV	Notes on Experience

(*1 = Very stressed/tired, 10 = Calm and energized)

Section 2: Journaling Prompts

Take 5-10 minutes to reflect on the following prompts:

1. **Body Awareness:** What physical sensations did you notice in your body today? Where did you feel tension, relaxation, or other sensations?

   _____

   _____

   _____

2. **Emotional State:** How did your emotions shift throughout the day? Did you notice any connection between your physical state and your emotions?

   _____

   _____

3. **Stress Management:** What somatic techniques worked best for you today? How did they help?

   _____

   _____

   _____

4. **Gratitude:** Write about one thing you appreciated about your body or how it helped you today.

_____

_____

_____

Section 3: Weekly Reflection

At the end of each week, take a moment to reflect on your progress:

1. **Wins:** What exercises or techniques worked best for you this week? How did they make you feel?

_____

_____

2. **Challenges:** Were there any days or techniques that felt more difficult? Why?

_____

3. **Adjustments:** What will you change or add to your routine next week?

_____

_____

4. **Overall Progress:** On a scale of 1-10, how much progress have you made this week in managing stress and improving emotional awareness?

_____

_____

Keep this tracker handy and fill it out daily. Consistency is key! Over time, you'll start seeing patterns in what helps you feel your best and how your practice builds emotional resilience. You've got this!

4

MANAGING HOPELESSNESS, DEPRESSION, & SELF-HARM URGES

"You don't have to control your thoughts. You just have to stop letting them control you."

— DAN MILLMAN

Important Note: Before You Read

If you're struggling with depression, self-harm urges, or feeling hopeless, please don't try to handle it all on your own. This book offers helpful tools but is **not a substitute for professional help**. When you're feeling down, it's easy to believe nothing will work or that you're beyond help—but **that's just the depression talking.** Your brain can play tricks on you, making it hard to see things clearly. That's why talking to a therapist, counselor, psychiatrist, or another trusted adult is so important. They can guide you through this in a way that keeps you safe and supported. Trying to fix everything yourself when you're struggling can worsen things, so please reach out. **You are not alone, and real help is out there.**

Life can feel totally overwhelming sometimes. Whether it's school stress, friend drama, family issues, or just feeling like everything's spinning out of control, those moments can hit hard. And when your mind is overloaded, your body feels it too. Somatic therapy is like a reset button for your mind and body, helping you handle the chaos without getting stuck in it.

During a crisis, your body is constantly sending you messages, like tight shoulders, a racing heart, or that sinking feeling in your stomach, to let you know something's off. Somatic therapy helps you listen to these signals and use them to find calm when everything feels overwhelming.

Somatic therapy gives your body a voice in your mental health journey. Your body acts like a memory bank that doesn't use words, and often, it's the first place where emotional stress shows up. While talking about what's bothering you is super important, somatic therapy goes deeper, helping you connect with what your body is holding onto—stress, anxiety, or even past experiences.

By learning to pay attention to these physical cues, you can understand what's going on beneath the surface and create a personalized toolkit for handling life's challenges. It's not just about fixing symptoms in the moment; it's about building long-term skills that help you feel more in control, even when life feels like a whirlwind.

RECOGNIZING SYMPTOMS OF EMOTIONAL CRISIS

Sometimes, life hits you so much at once that it feels like you're carrying a mountain. When things get tough emotionally, it doesn't just stay in your head—your whole body gets involved, too. Knowing the signs of an emotional crisis helps you figure out when to hit pause and take care of yourself.

Mental Symptoms

Ever feel like your brain is on a hamster wheel, running a million miles an hour? Overwhelming thoughts or a racing mind can make it hard to concentrate on anything, whether homework or just hanging out with friends. Persistent sadness or numbness—where everything feels blah—is another red flag. You might feel hopeless, like things won't get better no matter what you do.

Then there's that inner voice that loves to bring you down with self-criticism and negative self-talk, constantly telling you you're not good enough. Combine that with difficulty focusing or making even small decisions; it can feel like your brain's working against you. Frustration or irritability—snapping at people for no reason or feeling annoyed with yourself—is another sign that something's up emotionally.

Physical Symptoms

Sometimes, your body knows something's wrong before your brain does. Ever notice your hands clenching into fists, jaw tightening, or shoulders creeping up to your ears? That's muscle tension talking. Or maybe you feel restless, like you can't sit still, and your body's buzzing with this "on edge" energy. Conversely, fatigue or low energy can leave you feeling drained, even after a good night's sleep.

Other signs include an upset stomach, headaches, or random body aches that seem to pop up out of nowhere. Your sleep can also go haywire—either you can't fall asleep no matter how tired you are, or you're sleeping way more than usual but still feel wiped out. Sometimes, you might feel a sense of heaviness, like a weight on your chest, or a need for physical release, like pacing or fidgeting nonstop.

Recognizing these symptoms is a big deal because it's the first step to action. Your mind and body send you signals, and learning to listen to them is a form of self-care.

The Role of Body Awareness in a Crisis

Imagine that you're feeling overwhelmed but don't know why. Your thoughts are spinning, and you feel like you're on edge. Pause, take a deep breath, and notice what your body is trying to tell you. Maybe your chest feels tight, your hands are clammy, or your legs won't stop bouncing. These physical sensations are like little clues to what's happening emotionally.

By recognizing these signs, you can catch those overwhelming emotions before they spiral out of control. Body awareness is about being present—like hitting the "pause" button on a busy day—and tuning into your body's physical cues when you notice tension.

The best part? This sense of grounding and control can carry over into other parts of your life. The more you practice body awareness, the better you'll get at managing emotions, whether you're stressed about a test, dealing with friendship drama, or just having an off day. It's like having a secret weapon for emotional resilience—your body becomes your ally in tackling whatever comes your way.

Quick Mood Stabilizers for Emotional Crisis

Sometimes, life can feel like it's too much, and everything's happening simultaneously. Maybe your heart is racing, your thoughts are spiraling, or you feel like you're about to explode or shut down. When those moments hit, it's super important to have some quick tools you can pull out to help you feel more grounded and in control. Let's talk about three powerful somatic techniques you can use whenever you need to calm down fast.

Grounding Breath

Ever notice how your breathing changes when you're stressed? It gets faster and shallower, making you feel even more anxious. The grounding breath helps slow everything down and signals to your brain that you're safe, even if things feel chaotic.

Here's how to do it:

- Sit or stand somewhere comfortable. Place one hand on your chest and the other on your stomach.
- Take a deep breath through your nose for a count of four. Focus on making your stomach (not your chest) expand as you breathe.
- Hold your breath for a count of four.
- Slowly exhale through your mouth for a count of six, like you're blowing out a candle.
- Repeat this for at least 3–5 breaths.

You already know about heart rate variability (HRV) and how it measures your body's stress levels and ability to chill. This breathing technique is an awesome way to boost your HRV. By slowing your breathing and focusing on making your stomach expand, you're not just calming your mind—you're literally teaching your body to relax and find balance.

Think of it like a workout for your nervous system. Each breath is helping your HRV improve, which means you're better equipped to handle whatever comes your way. Your heart rate slows, your brain clears, and it's like you've just flipped a switch from "stressed out" to "ready to handle it."

Whether you're preparing for a test, gearing up for a game, or managing a tough moment, this technique is a quick and effective way to stay in control—and keep your HRV in the healthy zone.

Body Awareness Tapping

When you feel like you're freaking out, your thoughts can feel like they're spinning out of control. Body awareness tapping shifts your focus from those overwhelming thoughts to your physical body. It's simple, but it works.

Here's how to do it:

- Use your fingertips to gently tap different body parts, like your collarbone, thighs, or the sides of your hands.
- As you tap, pay attention to the sensation. Feel the rhythm and notice the connection to your body.
- You can say something soothing to yourself, like, "I'm okay," or count the taps out loud to help you stay present.
- Keep tapping for a few minutes until you feel your mind quiet down and your body relax.

Body Awareness Tapping doesn't just help you feel grounded—it can also work wonders for your HRV. You've learned that HRV is like a health meter for your stress levels, and tapping can help you nudge it in the right direction. As you focus on the rhythm of the taps and the sensations in your body, you're calming your nervous system, which helps balance your HRV.

Want to take it a step further? If you've got a smartwatch or HRV tracker, try checking your HRV before and after tapping. You might notice it starts to improve as your body relaxes and your stress fades. It's like a real-time progress report for how much chill you've gained! Whether or not you're tracking, know that each tap is helping your body and mind find balance—one small step at a time.

Sensory Reset

Engaging your senses can help when your emotions run wild. The sensory reset technique shifts your focus to the physical world around you, helping you break free from the overwhelm.

Here's how it works:

- **Touch:** Hold something with texture—like a soft blanket, a stress ball, or even your phone case—and focus on how it feels in your hands. Is it smooth, rough, warm, or cool?
  - **Sound:** Put on a song that makes you feel calm or happy. Close your eyes and listen to the instruments, the beat, and the lyrics.
  - **Smell:** Sniff something soothing, like lavender oil, a scented candle, or even a piece of gum. Scents can calm the brain almost instantly.
  - **Sight:** Look around and name five things you can see. Bonus points if you notice colors, patterns, or tiny details you'd usually overlook.
  - **Taste:** Pop a piece of gum, candy, or a snack in your mouth. Focus on the flavor and how it feels on your tongue.

The sensory reset technique doesn't just help calm your emotions—it's also a great way to support your HRV. When you focus on touch, sound, smell, sight, or taste, you're activating your parasympathetic nervous system—the part of your body responsible for rest and relaxation. This shift helps balance your HRV, making your body feel less "on edge" and more at ease.

Check your HRV before and after a sensory reset if you have an HRV tracker or smartwatch. You might notice that as your brain and body chill out, your HRV improves, showing that this simple technique really works.

Each of these exercises helps interrupt the stress response in your body. They're fast and easy; you can do them anywhere—at your desk, in the bathroom, or while walking between classes.

The best thing about these techniques is how easily they adapt to your day. Do you feel panicked before giving a class presentation? Use grounding breath. Do you feel restless in a study group? Try body awareness tapping under the table. Are you stressed out during a team huddle? Focus on a quick sensory reset by holding your water bottle and noticing its texture.

With these tools, you don't have to wait until you're at home or in a private space to care for yourself. They're designed to be quick, easy, and portable. You can do them anywhere, anytime, without anyone even noticing.

MINDFUL BODY AWARENESS TO EASE HOPELESSNESS

Hopelessness isn't just sadness—it's deeper, like a sense of purposelessness that settles in your chest. It might show up as thoughts like:

- "What's the point of even trying?"
- "I'll never be good enough."
- "Nothing ever changes for me."

You might feel like you're on autopilot, just going through the motions but not living. Or maybe you're overwhelmed, like you've hit a wall, and there's no way to climb over it. This mental fog can leave you feeling like you're stuck, lost, and carrying a heavy weight you can't put down.

Hopelessness can show up for a lot of reasons. Maybe school has been rough, or you've had trouble at home. It might stem from pressure to meet expectations from parents, teachers, or even yourself. When things pile up, it's easy to feel like there's no way forward.

Feeling stuck doesn't mean you *are* stuck. Hopelessness is like a trick your brain plays when overwhelmed—it makes you focus on what's going wrong instead of seeing the possibilities for what can go right. Recognizing these feelings is the first step toward breaking free from them.

Physical Symptoms of Hopelessness

Hopelessness doesn't just mess with your emotions; it can also take a toll on your body. When hopelessness sets in, it can show up in ways you might not even realize.

Low Energy

Have you ever felt completely drained, even though you didn't do anything physically exhausting? That's one of the biggest physical signs of hopelessness. It's like your body is in slow motion, and even simple things—like getting out of bed or walking to class—feel like a huge effort. No matter how much sleep you get, you feel tired because hopelessness zaps your energy.

Slumped Posture

When you're feeling hopeless, your posture often reflects it. You might notice your shoulders rounding forward, your head hanging low, or your whole body slouching. This isn't just about looking sad—it's your body's way of mirroring how heavy everything feels inside. It's like carrying an invisible weight that drags you down.

Reduced Motivation

Hopelessness can make your body feel like it's on strike. That drive to do things you once enjoyed? Gone. It feels pointless, whether it's hitting the gym, going for a walk, or even something as simple as stretching. Your muscles feel heavy, and it's hard to muster up the energy to move.

DEFINING MINDFUL BODY AWARENESS

Mindful body awareness is like taking a break from life's chaos and tuning into what's happening in your body. By paying attention to the little sensations—like how your chest feels when you breathe or where tension sits in your muscles—you can get a better grip on your emotions. It's a simple, powerful way to understand your feelings and take steps to feel better, especially when hopelessness creeps in.

Let's explore some cool, easy-to-do techniques to help you tap into this awareness and turn things around.

Mindful Breathing With Positive Intention

Breathing might seem basic—it's something you do without thinking—but adding mindfulness and affirmations can change the game. Here's how:

- **Find Your Spot:** Sit or lie down somewhere comfy. If you're at school or on the go, find a quiet moment.
- **Breathe Deep:** Take a slow, deep breath through your nose for four counts, letting your belly expand. Then, exhale through your mouth for six counts.
- **Add Positivity:** As you inhale, think, or say to yourself, "I am capable." When you exhale, think or say, "I release hopelessness."
- **Repeat:** Do this for a few minutes, focusing on the rhythm of your breath and your words.

Mindful breathing with positive intention isn't just about chilling out—it's like a power-up for your HRV. When you breathe slow and steady and add some positive vibes, you're actually training your body to handle stress better.

Here's the cool part—that long exhale you're doing? It activates your chill mode (a.k.a. your parasympathetic nervous system), which gives your HRV a boost and tells your body, "Hey, it's all good." If you've got an HRV tracker, you might even see your numbers start to improve as your heart rate steadies and your body relaxes. Each breath you take helps your body and brain remember that you've got this. So, the next time life feels overwhelming, grab a few minutes for this practice. You're not just breathing—you're building up your inner strength and showing your body who's boss.

Body Scan for Emotional Recognition

A body scan is like taking a tour of yourself to figure out where you're holding onto stress or sadness. It's perfect for those moments when despair feels overwhelming.

- **Get Comfortable:** Lie down or sit in a quiet spot. Close your eyes if it feels right.
- **Start at Your Head:** Pay attention to your forehead, jaw, and neck. Notice if you're clenching or holding tension there.
- **Move Down:** Slowly shift your focus to your shoulders, chest, stomach, and legs, all the way to your toes.
- **Acknowledge and Release:** Imagine breathing into that spot when you notice tightness or discomfort. Picture the tension leaving your body as you exhale.
- **Reflect:** At the end, ask yourself, "What emotions were tied to those sensations?" This can help you connect physical feelings to your emotional state.

This simple practice does more than just help you feel better in the moment. By releasing tension and calming your body, you're giving your HRV a boost.

If you want to go to the next level, try pairing this with some light exercise. Moving your body—like stretching or walking afterward—helps release any left-over tension and keeps your HRV on the rise. It's like giving your body and brain a full reboot, leaving you feeling more connected, calm, and ready to take on whatever comes your way.

Supportive Self-Hug

Yeah, it might sound cheesy, but a self-hug can be surprisingly comforting. It's a simple way to show yourself some love when things get tough.

- **Cross Your Arms:** Wrap them around like you're giving yourself a big bear hug.
- **Squeeze Gently:** Add a little pressure to feel secure and held.
- **Breathe and Ground:** Take a few deep breaths as you hold yourself. Remind yourself, "I've got my own back."
- **Optional Movement:** Rock gently side to side if it feels soothing.

This small action creates a sense of safety and calm, reminding you that you're not alone—you've got you. The pressure and movement signal your body to relax, which can lower stress levels, make you feel more grounded, and help improve your HRV.

Mindful body awareness helps you recognize what's happening inside, gives you tools to respond, and helps you start feeling better, one step at a time. Sure, it might take practice, but each time you try these exercises, you're taking control of your emotions and proving that hopelessness doesn't get to win.

RECOGNIZING SYMPTOMS OF DEPRESSION

Before we dive in, it's really important to say this: **If you think you might be dealing with depression, don't try to figure it out alone.** Depression is more than just a bad mood; it affects how your brain works, and it can make it hard to see things clearly. A professional, like a therapist or doctor, can help you understand what's really going on and find the right support for you. They're trained to guide you through it and ensure you get the help you need. Trying to push through on your own or hoping it will go away can make things harder in the long run. **You deserve real support, and reaching out to a professional is one of the strongest, most important things you can do for yourself.**

Depression isn't just feeling sad—it's a deep, complex experience that affects both your mind and body. It can feel like carrying around an invisible weight that no one else sees or understands. Some days, it might show up as a sadness that just won't go away, even if there's no obvious reason for it. Other times, it feels like a complete lack of motivation. Activities you used to love—whether it's hanging out with friends, playing sports, or watching your favorite shows—might not bring you any joy anymore. Even simple things, like brushing your teeth or finishing a school project, can feel as impossible as climbing Mount Everest.

What Depression Does to Your Mind

Depression can fog up your mind like a cloudy day that never clears. Concentrating on homework, remembering what you studied, or even making simple decisions like what to eat for lunch might feel overwhelming. Your brain feels like it is stuck in slow motion, making everything harder than it used to be.

And then there's the emptiness—that feeling like there's a hole inside you that nothing can fill. Even when good things happen, it's tough to enjoy them. You might also notice an increase in negative thoughts, like "I'm not good enough," "I can't do anything right," or "Why can't I just feel better already?" These thoughts can feel relentless, and it's easy to believe them, even though they're not true.

The Body's Response to Depression

Depression doesn't just live in your head—it takes a toll on your body, too. Fatigue is a big one. You might feel constantly drained, no matter how much you sleep. Waking up in the morning might feel like the hardest part of your day, and even after a full night's rest, your energy levels might still be at zero.

You could also feel physical tension, like your muscles are wound up tight and never fully relax. Headaches might pop up out of nowhere, or you might feel heaviness throughout your entire body like gravity turned up and everything is harder to move. Even your appetite can change—some days, you might not feel like eating at all, while on others, you might crave comfort foods.

The Mind-Body Connection of Depression

We know that the mind and body are deeply connected. It makes sense that when your brain is overwhelmed, your body reacts—tight muscles, fatigue, and physical aches are all signs of this connection. It's like your brain and body are shouting, "Hey, we need help here!"

Knowing this doesn't make the feelings disappear, but it can help you realize that depression isn't your fault. You're not "weak" or "broken" because you feel this way. Depression is a real challenge, and understanding the symptoms is the first step toward feeling better.

Why Recognizing the Symptoms Matters

Besides giving your feelings a name, recognizing these signs helps you know that you're not alone and that what you're going through is valid. Many people, including teens like you, experience depression, and it doesn't mean there's something wrong with you. It means you're human.

The good news? There are ways to address these symptoms. Talking to someone you trust, like a parent, teacher, or counselor, can be the first step. Somatic therapy techniques, like deep breathing and grounding exercises, can help you feel more connected to your body and ease some of the tension. You don't have to navigate this alone—help is out there, and healing is possible.

Breaking Free From Depression With Somatic Therapy

When you're feeling down, getting up and moving might be the last thing on your mind. But here's the thing: Physical activity isn't just about staying fit. Movement helps your body release endorphins, those feel-good chemicals that are basically your brain's natural pick-me-ups. Plus, it's a great way to release tension, clear your head, and even boost your HRV, which is a fancy way of saying it helps your body handle stress better.

And guess what! You don't need to do intense workouts to feel the benefits. Gentle, intentional movement can make a huge difference in lifting your mood and reconnecting with your body. Here are some simple somatic techniques to try:

Stretch and Shake

Start with a few easy stretches—reach for the sky, lean side to side, roll your shoulders, or stretch your arms wide like you're making wings. Then, shake it out! Shake your hands, arms, legs, and even your head if it feels good. It might feel silly at first, but that's kind of the point. Let yourself laugh and loosen up. Shaking helps release pent-up energy and tension, leaving you feeling lighter and more awake.

Dynamic Body Movement

Think freestyle dancing—no rules, no judgments, just movement. Put on your favorite song and let your body take over. Sway, jump, spin, or stomp. This isn't about

looking cool; it's about feeling free and letting go of the weight you've been carrying. Moving in your own unique way helps you process emotions and shift your focus away from negative thoughts.

Slow Walking Meditation

Forget rushing to your next class or power walking for exercise—this is about walking with intention. Take slow, steady steps, and notice how your feet connect with the ground. Feel the texture under your shoes, the rhythm of your breath, and the sounds around you. This simple practice can clear your mind and help you feel more present, calm, and steady.

Progressive Muscle Release

Try tensing and relaxing different parts of your body. Start with your toes—curl them tightly, hold for a few seconds, and then release. Move up to your legs, then your arms, shoulders, and even your face. This technique helps you notice where you're holding tension and gives you a satisfying sense of release.

Wall Pushes or Resistance Moves

Stand facing a wall and press your hands into it as hard as you can for a few seconds, then release. You can also do this by pressing your palms together or gripping the edges of a chair. These moves give your body the physical release it craves, like channeling all that bottled-up energy into something productive and safe.

Why Movement Matters

These exercises aren't about being perfect or turning into a fitness fanatic. They're about giving your body and mind a break when you're feeling overwhelmed. Even just a few minutes of movement can help shift your mood and bring a little lightness back into your day.

When you make movement a regular habit, even in small doses, it's like building a superpower for handling tough emotions. It doesn't have to be complicated— stretch while watching a show, shake it out between homework assignments, or walk to clear your head after school. These little moments of movement add up, helping you feel more balanced and in control over time.

Non-Movement Somatic Techniques

Body Scan Meditation

Lie down or sit in a quiet space and slowly focus on each part of your body, starting at your head and working down to your toes. Notice any tension or discomfort, and imagine breathing into those spots. This technique helps you identify where you're holding stress and depression and gently release it.

Grounding with Touch

Place your hands on your heart, wrap your arms around yourself in a self-hug, or press your palms together firmly. These grounding touches can help you feel safe, steady, and connected to your body, especially during moments of emotional overwhelm and depression.

Sensory Engagement

Focus on your senses to pull yourself into the present. Hold something textured, like a blanket or stress ball, and pay attention to how it feels. Look around and name five things you can see. Smell something calming, like lavender oil, or put on music that soothes you. These sensory techniques help ground you and ease the mental fog that often comes with depression.

Why These Techniques Work

All these techniques share one powerful benefit: They help you reconnect with your body when your mind feels overwhelmed. Depression often creates a disconnect between your emotions and physical self, making it hard to feel present or in control. Somatic therapy bridges that gap, giving you tools to ground yourself, release tension, and shift your focus.

Consistency Is Key

Just like brushing your teeth or charging your phone, these techniques work best when practiced regularly. You don't need to do them all at once—choose one or two that resonate with you and make them part of your day. Maybe it's stretching in the morning, a body scan before bed, or squeezing a stress ball during a tough moment.

The more you practice, the more you'll notice how these small actions can lift your mood, steady your emotions, and help you feel more balanced overall. Depression doesn't define you—it's just one part of your story. With these tools, you're building resilience and proving to yourself that you've got what it takes to navigate even the hardest days. And that's something worth celebrating.

TECHNIQUES FOR SELF-HARM URGES

Sometimes, life can feel like too much, and your mind can get so overwhelmed that it's hard to see a way out. When things get heavy, thoughts can start racing, frustration builds up, and self-criticism takes over. It might feel like you're stuck in a loop of negativity, and those overwhelming emotions don't seem to have a way out. That's when the idea of self-harm can sneak in—not because you want to hurt yourself but because you're desperately trying to cope with everything inside.

Mental symptoms tied to self-harm often include feeling trapped by over-whelming thoughts or emotions. You might hear that inner critic way louder than usual, pointing out everything you think you've done wrong. Frustration can boil over, making it feel like there's no other way to release your feelings. It's a lot, and if this sounds familiar, please know that you're not alone—lots of people have been there, and there's help to get through it.

Physical self-harm urges can show up as intense tension in your body. Maybe your hands feel clenched or restless, like they need to do something, or your jaw feels tight from holding in emotions. You might even feel like you have this energy building up inside that has nowhere to go—a need for a release to quiet the storm.

It is important to remember that these feelings, as overwhelming as they are, don't have to control you. Recognizing these signs—both mental and physical—is a huge step. When you notice these triggers and urges, you're opening the door to finding healthier ways to cope.

Somatic Techniques to Substitute Self-Harm

When everything feels overwhelming, it's important to remember that there are ways to release those intense emotions and physical urges without harming yourself. Your body craves a sense of relief during tough moments, and somatic techniques can help you find that release safely while calming your mind. Let's explore a few methods that can help substitute self-harm with healthier, body-centered alternatives.

Cold Water Reset

When everything feels like too much, cold water can be a powerful ally. It uses a physical sensation to calm your brain and body in moments of intense emotion. Here's the science behind it: Cold water activates your dive reflex, a natural response in your body that slows your heart rate and shifts you into a calmer state. It's your body's way of saying, "Hey, let's take a breather."

Here's how you can try it:

- **Wrist Dip:** Fill a bowl with cold water and dip your wrists into it for 30 seconds to a minute. The skin on your wrists is sensitive, so the cold sensation grabs your attention and helps redirect those intense urges.
- **Face Splash:** Splashing cold water on your face isn't just refreshing—it can also help calm that storm of emotions in your head. Close your eyes, take a deep breath, and feel the water bring you back to the present moment.
- **Ice Pack or Ice Cube:** If you don't have access to water, grab an ice pack or even a few ice cubes. Hold them in your hand, press them against your

wrists, or place them on the back of your neck. The chill helps ground you, giving your mind and body a chance to reset.

Cold water doesn't just feel calming—it can also improve your HRV. When you use cold water, you're helping your nervous system find balance, making it easier over time to regain control and feel steady again.

Give it a try the next time those self-harm urges creep in. You might be surprised by how effective this simple technique can be. It's not about being perfect—it's about finding ways to take care of yourself, one step at a time. You've got what it takes to face those tough moments and come out stronger. Every time you choose a healthier alternative, you're proving to yourself that you can handle it—and that's something to be proud of.

Stress Ball or Hand Squeeze

Sometimes, it feels like your emotions are too big to hold inside, and your hands crave something to do with all that restless energy. That's where a stress ball comes in—it's like a tiny tool of relief that fits right in your hand. Squeezing a stress ball gives you a safe, physical way to channel those overwhelming feelings and create a release without harm.

Here's why it works: When you clench your hands around the ball and then release, you're mimicking the natural tension-and-release cycle your muscles go through during physical stress. This action sends a calming signal to your brain, letting it know you're in control. It's kind of like your body saying, "We've got this." If you don't have a stress ball, no problem—just clench your fists tight for a few seconds, then release. You can even grab something firm, like a rolled-up towel, for the same effect.

The benefits go beyond just releasing tension. Squeezing something gives your body a focal point for all that energy, grounding you in the moment and pulling you out of overwhelming thoughts. Plus, it's satisfying to physically feel the tension leave your body as your hands relax. This small, repetitive action helps your mind slow down and reconnect with the present, making it easier to ride out those intense feelings without hurting yourself.

Using a stress ball can also help improve your HRV. As your body relaxes, your HRV increases, showing that you're bouncing back and finding balance. Next time the urge to self-harm creeps in, reach for a stress ball or clench your fists and release. It's a simple, effective way to show your body kindness and remind yourself that you're in control. You're stronger than those tough moments, and every time you choose a healthier outlet, you're proving to yourself that you can get through it—and that's a huge win.

Grounding Touch

When the urge to self-harm feels overwhelming, grounding yourself through touch can be a game changer. It's about using a physical connection to bring your focus back to the present moment and remind yourself that you're in control. One easy technique is gently pressing your palms together, creating a steady sense of pressure. Another is wrapping your hands around your forearms or shoulders in a comforting grip, like a self-hug. You can also try placing your hand over your heart or applying gentle pressure to your arms—find what feels right for you.

Here's why it works: These simple actions help you reconnect with your body, giving you something safe and tangible to focus on. The sensation of touch, especially when firm and steady, activates your parasympathetic nervous system, the part of your body that helps calm you down. It sends your brain a message: "I'm here, I'm safe, and I'm in control."

The benefits go beyond just feeling grounded. Techniques like these can satisfy your body's craving for physical release without harm. That steady pressure helps soothe racing thoughts and can improve your HRV by calming your nervous system. When your HRV rises, it means your body is bouncing back from stress, helping you feel more balanced and capable.

The best part about grounding touch techniques is that they are quick, discreet, and always available. You can use them at school, at home, or even when you're out with friends, and no one has to know. They're not just substitutes for self-harm—they're tools that empower you to take back control and show yourself compassion in those tough moments. Every time you use these techniques, you're making a choice to care for yourself, proving that you can navigate the hard times with strength and kindness. It's a powerful step toward healing!

Download your interactive chapter worksheets *NOW* to apply these techniques, track your progress, and build real emotional resilience—one step at a time.

SCAN QR CODE FOR DOWNLOADABLE WORKSHEETS

INTERACTIVE WORKSHEET

Use these prompts to reflect on your emotions and bodily experiences. Write at least one entry per day.

Beginning HRV: _____ Ending HRV: Baseline HRV: _____

1. Note any trends you are noticing in your HRV.

_____

2. How am I feeling right now? Describe your emotions in detail.

_____

_____

3. What physical sensations am I noticing in my body? (e.g., tension, warmth, heaviness)

_____

_____

4. What triggered these emotions or sensations? (e.g., a conversation, a memory, a stressful event)

----

5. What somatic exercise did I try today? How did it make me feel?

----

6. What is one thing I can do to support myself right now?

Crisis-Specific Techniques Reflection

Date: _____

1. Technique used: (e.g., cold water reset, stress ball squeeze, grounding touch)

----

2. Why did you use this technique? (e.g., to reduce anxiety, stop overwhelming thoughts, stabilize emotions)

----

3. What was happening when you used this technique?

_____

_____

4. What emotions or urges were you experiencing?

_____

_____

5. Did the technique help you feel calmer or more in control?

_____

_____

6. How long did it take to feel a difference?

_____

_____

7. What will you remember to do next time?

_____

_____

TRAUMA-INFORMED SOMATIC PRACTICES

"The body remembers what the mind forgets."

— BESSEL VAN DER KOLK

Trauma might sound like a heavy word, but it's something many teens experience, whether they realize it or not. At its core, trauma happens when you go through something overwhelming—something that shakes you to the core and makes you feel unsafe or out of control. This could be an obvious, sudden event like an accident, the loss of someone close to you, or experiencing bullying. But trauma can also build up over time, like feeling constant pressure at home, ongoing stress at school, or dealing with complicated friendships and relationships.

However, you're not alone if you've faced tough situations that stick with you. Studies suggest that about 60% of teens have experienced some trauma before they even turn 18. That's a lot of people! Whether it's something personal or something happening in the world around you, trauma can have a big impact on your emotional and mental health. It can show up as anxiety, difficulty trusting others, or even physical symptoms like headaches or stomachaches.

It doesn't always look the same for everyone if you've been through something traumatic. Some signs to watch out for in yourself or your friends include:

- Feeling more irritable or angry than usual
- Zoning out or avoiding certain places or people
- Trouble sleeping or having bad dreams
- Always feeling on edge, like something terrible is about to happen
- Pulling away from friends and family
- Struggling to focus in class or on homework

These aren't just random feelings—they could be your body and mind's way of responding to something you've been through.

Knowing you don't have to deal with it alone is super important if you're feeling this way. The earlier you or the people around you recognize the effects of trauma, the easier it is to start feeling better. Talking to someone you trust—a parent, teacher, therapist, counselor, or friend—can make all the difference.

For parents, early intervention means paying attention to changes in mood or behavior and offering support without judgment. This could look like listening more than lecturing, giving teens space to open up, or even suggesting professional help.

HOW TRAUMA AFFECTS THE BODY AND MIND

Trauma doesn't just live in your memories—it has a way of settling into your body, too. When you experience something overwhelming, your body kicks into survival mode. Your heart races, your breathing quickens, and your muscles tense up, all thanks to your nervous system reacting to protect you. This is totally normal in the moment, but sometimes, your body doesn't fully "turn off" that survival mode, even after the danger or stress has passed.

That's why trauma can leave you feeling stuck. Your mind might want to move on, but your body could still be carrying the stress, almost like it's frozen in time. You might notice it in unexpected ways—maybe your shoulders always feel tight, or you get headaches or stomachaches for no obvious reason. Even zoning out or feeling disconnected from the world can be your body's way of coping with the leftover tension.

Healing from trauma isn't just about talking through what happened (though that's important, too). It's also about helping your body feel safe again. That's where somatic therapy comes in—it focuses on using your body to help calm your mind. This connection is especially important for dealing with PTSD or complex trauma, which can make your body feel like it's constantly on high alert.

By practicing techniques that gently engage your body, like mindful movements or grounding exercises, you can start to retrain your nervous system. You need to teach your body that it's okay to relax, step by step. This teamwork between your mind and body is a powerful part of the healing process, and the best part is that it's something you can learn and practice, even during the toughest times.

BLENDING TALK AND SOMATIC THERAPY FOR TRAUMA

If you've been through trauma and tried talking about it in therapy, you might have felt like something was still missing. Maybe you've done all the right things —opened up about your experiences, explored your feelings, and worked on changing your thoughts—but you still feel stuck. That's because, as we have pointed out, trauma doesn't just live in your mind; it also shows up in your body. And if the physical side of trauma isn't addressed, it can keep holding you back, no matter how much progress you make mentally.

While talk therapy focuses on your thoughts and emotions, somatic therapy adds another layer by helping your body heal from the trauma it's been holding onto. Think of it like this: Your mind might understand that the danger is over, but your body might still feel like it's in survival mode. That's why you might notice tight muscles, random aches, or a sense of always being on edge—even if your brain knows you're safe.

By combining somatic therapy with talk therapy, you can approach trauma recovery from both angles. For example, you might talk to your therapist about a triggering situation and then use a grounding technique, like the 5-4-3-2-1 method, to calm the physical response that comes with reliving those emotions. Or, after a tough therapy session, you could try some gentle movements, like shoulder rolls or body tapping, to release any tension that built up in your body during the conversation.

Somatic therapy also helps you reconnect with your body in a safe and empowering way. Trauma can make you feel disconnected from yourself, almost like you're numb or out of touch with your own feelings. Somatic exercises, like deep breathing or grounding techniques, help bridge that gap, giving you a sense of control over your body again.

For teens especially, this mind-body connection can make a huge difference. You're in a stage of life where emotions and experiences can feel overwhelming, and combining somatic therapy with talk therapy gives you more tools to handle it all. It's not about replacing one with the other—it's about giving yourself a fuller, more balanced approach to healing.

If you've felt stuck in your trauma recovery, know that it's not your fault. Sometimes, the missing piece is addressing what your body has been carrying. With the help of somatic therapy and a supportive therapist, you can start to release those physical effects of trauma and move forward with a sense of safety and strength. It's not an instant fix, but every step you take toward feeling better—mentally and physically—is progress worth celebrating.

SOMATIC TECHNIQUES FOR TRAUMA RECOVERY

If you've been through something tough, healing can feel like an uphill climb. The good news is that your body can be a powerful ally in that process. Somatic exercises are all about using gentle, mindful movements and techniques to help you feel safer and more connected to yourself. The key is starting small and listening to what your body needs.

Gentle Movement Exercises

When you've experienced trauma, your body might hold onto tension or stress without you even realizing it. Gentle movements can help release some of that built-up tension without feeling overwhelmed.

Try these:

Slow Shoulder Roll

- Sit or stand in a comfortable spot.
- Slowly shrug your shoulders up toward your ears.
- Roll them back and down in a smooth circle.
- Repeat a few times and notice how your body feels.

This kind of slight, intentional movement can help your body start to relax without pushing it too far.

Grounded Foot Tapping

- Sit in a chair with your feet flat on the floor.
- Gently tap one foot against the ground, then the other, like you're creating a slow rhythm.
- Focus on the connection between your feet and the floor as you tap.

This rhythmic motion can help your body feel more connected to the earth and less overwhelmed.

Sensory Grounding Techniques

Trauma can make you feel disconnected from the present moment. Sensory grounding techniques bring you back into the here and now by focusing on what your senses pick up. Here are some easy methods:

5-4-3-2-1 Technique

- Look around and name 5 things you can see.
- Touch 4 things around you (a soft pillow, your jeans, a pet).

- Listen for 3 different sounds.
- Smell 2 scents (your shampoo or even just fresh air).
- Notice 1 thing you can taste (chew gum or sip water).

These steps help shift your focus from overwhelming emotions to what's happening around you, which can be super grounding.

Temperature Awareness

- Hold an ice cube or dip your fingers into cold water.
- Pay attention to the chill and how it feels on your skin.
- Notice how the sensation shifts your focus from your thoughts to the physical world.

This method works quickly to bring your mind back to the present and calm intense emotions.

Breathwork Techniques

Belly Breathing

When you're dealing with tough stuff, it can feel like your body is stuck in over-drive. That's where belly breathing—also known as diaphragmatic breathing—comes in. It's the best breathing technique to help you feel calmer, more grounded, and in control.

1. **Find a safe spot.** Sit or lie down somewhere you feel secure. Place one hand on your chest and the other on your belly.
2. **Breathe in deep.** Take a slow, deep breath in through your nose. Let your belly rise like a balloon filling with air. Keep your chest still.
3. **Breathe out slowly.** Exhale through your mouth, feeling your belly sink back down.

4. **Set a rhythm**. Try inhaling for 4 seconds, holding for 2, and exhaling for 6. Take your time—it's not a race.

Why Belly Breathing Works for Trauma

- **It tells your body to chill.** Belly breathing activates your vagus nerve, which sends a message to your body that it's safe to relax.
- **It grounds you in the moment.** Trauma can leave you feeling disconnected or like you're floating outside yourself. Focusing on your breath brings you back to the present and helps you feel steadier.
- **It keeps emotions manageable.** Deep breathing balances your nervous system, making those big, overwhelming feelings easier to handle.

Other Breathing Tricks for Trauma

- **Resonance Breathing**: Breathe in and out slowly, aiming for about 5 or 6 breaths per minute. This helps your body find its natural calm.
- **Box Breathing**: Imagine drawing a box with your breath. Inhale for 4 seconds, hold for 4, exhale for 4, and hold again for 4. It's a great way to refocus when you're feeling overwhelmed.
- **Humming Breath**: Breathe in deeply through your nose, and hum softly as you exhale. The vibrations activate your vagus nerve, which helps calm your body and mind and gives you a sense of safety.

TAKE IT ONE STEP AT A TIME

If you're working through trauma, it's okay to start small. A few breaths here and there can make a big difference. If it feels too much, pair your breathing with grounding techniques, like holding something soft or focusing on a soothing sound.

Belly breathing isn't just a tool for calming down in the moment—it's a way to take back control and remind your body that you're safe. Keep practicing, and you'll find it gets easier to handle whatever life throws your way.

Body Awareness Exercises

When trauma makes you feel disconnected from your body, exercises that increase awareness can help.

Body Tapping

- Use your fingertips to gently tap different parts of your body, like your arms, legs, or chest.
- Focus on the sensation of the tapping and how it connects you to your physical self.

Palm Pressure

- Place one hand over the other and press them together gently.
- Focus on the warmth and pressure as your hands connect.

These small actions can help you feel grounded and remind you that you're in control of your body.

Progressive Muscle Relaxation for Trauma Recovery

When you're dealing with trauma, your body might feel like it's constantly bracing for impact—tense and on edge. Progressive muscle relaxation (PMR) is a somatic technique that helps you gently release that tension by focusing on one muscle group at a time. It's like giving your body permission to let go, step by step.

Here's how to try PMR:

1. **Find a comfortable spot.** Sit or lie down in a place where you feel safe and relaxed. Close your eyes if it feels okay.
2. **Focus on one muscle group.** Start with your feet. Curl your toes tightly and hold for about 5 seconds. Notice the tension.
3. **Release the tension.** Let go of the tension all at once and focus on the sensation of your muscles relaxing.
4. **Move up your body.** Work your way through each muscle group—your calves, thighs, stomach, shoulders, arms, and even your face.
   - For your shoulders, shrug them up toward your ears and then let them drop.
   - For your hands, clench your fists, then release.
5. **Take your time.** Spend a few moments noticing how each part of your body feels after you've released the tension.

PMR helps you reconnect with your body and sends signals to your nervous system that it's safe to relax. It's especially helpful during moments of high stress or when you're trying to wind down after a tough day.

Pendulation for Trauma Recovery

Pendulation is a gentle technique that helps you balance between feelings of discomfort and safety, allowing your body to process trauma without becoming overwhelmed. It requires learning to move back and forth—like a pendulum—between challenging sensations and calm, grounded states.

Here's how to practice pendulation:

1. **Start in a grounded state.** Focus on something that feels calming or safe,

like your breath, the sensation of your feet on the ground, or a comforting object nearby.

2. **Notice a discomfort.** Shift your attention to a part of your body that feels tense or uneasy, such as a tightness in your chest or a knot in your stomach.

3. **Stay present.** Instead of trying to fix or change the sensation, just notice it. Remind yourself that it's okay to feel this way—it's just your body's way of processing.

4. **Return to safety.** After a few moments, shift your focus back to the grounded state you started with. This could be your breath, the floor under your feet, or the warmth of your hands.

5. **Repeat the cycle.** Go back and forth a few times, spending a little longer in the calm state each time.

Pendulation helps you build resilience by teaching your body that it's possible to explore discomfort without being stuck in it. It gives you a roadmap to navigate tough emotions safely.

These techniques, like PMR and pendulation, work alongside other somatic practices to help you reconnect with your body, process emotions, and find moments of relief.

COMBINING TECHNIQUES

You can mix and match these techniques to find what works best for you. You might pair box breathing with body tapping or follow a sensory grounding exercise with gentle movement. The goal is to experiment and discover what helps you feel calmer and more connected to yourself.

Healing from trauma takes time, but these somatic techniques can help you along the way. Each small step you take toward feeling safer in your body is a win, and you deserve to celebrate that progress. You've got this!

THE GRADUAL PROCESS OF HEALING

Healing from trauma isn't a sprint—it's more like a slow, steady walk. Somatic therapy respects your pace, letting you heal one step at a time. If an exercise feels like too much, pause or modify it. Over time, as you build trust with your body, you might find you can do more. The goal is progress, not perfection.

Pacing and Progression

Start with what feels manageable. If five minutes of a grounding exercise is all you can handle today, that's a win. Over time, those five minutes might turn into ten, and you'll notice yourself feeling stronger and more in control.

Body Awareness

Trauma often hides in the body, showing up as tight muscles, aches, or a sense of being "on edge." Body awareness helps you recognize and work through these signs instead of letting them weigh you down.

One way to start body awareness is with a simple body scan:

- Find a quiet place where you won't be interrupted.

- Close your eyes (if you feel comfortable) and take a deep breath.
- Slowly bring your attention to each body part, starting with your toes and moving upward. Notice any areas of tension, warmth, or even numbness.
- Take a moment to acknowledge how you feel without judgment.

The more you practice, the more you'll notice patterns—like how your jaw might clench when you're stressed or your shoulders tense up during tough moments. Recognizing these signs gives you the power to address them.

As you build this connection with your body, you might find that the emotions you've been holding onto start to surface. That's normal. Let your body guide you through the process at the right pace. You're learning to listen to yourself, which is a huge step toward healing.

THE CONNECTION BETWEEN TRIGGERS AND TRAUMA

Triggers and trauma are closely linked. When you've experienced something traumatic, your brain stores the memory of what happened and the emotions and sensations that came with it. When something reminds your brain of that event, even vaguely, it reacts like it's happening all over again. Understanding triggers gives you the power to recognize what's happening and take steps to feel more in control.

Safely Navigating Emotional Triggers

Trauma isn't just about what happened in the past. It can show up out of nowhere, hijacking your emotions in the middle of your day. These moments, when something suddenly stirs up overwhelming feelings connected to an experience, are called *emotional triggers.*

Emotional triggers are like landmines—something in your environment, like a sound, smell, or even a specific situation, "sets off" a strong emotional reaction.

These reactions can be tied to past trauma, often without you even realizing it. If you've been through something scary, a loud noise or a raised voice might send your heart racing. This is your brain's way of trying to protect you by reacting to something that feels unsafe, even if the danger isn't real this time.

Common Triggers for Teens

As a teen, you're juggling a lot: school, friendships, family, and figuring out who you are. This makes some triggers more common for you than for adults. Here are a few examples:

- Arguments or criticism from teachers, parents, or peers
- Social media comparisons or bullying
- Certain dates or anniversaries tied to past events
- Feeling excluded or rejected in social situations

Learn to recognize your triggers. You might be triggered if you notice your heart racing, your chest feeling tight, or your thoughts spinning after a certain event or situation. Pay attention to your body—it often tells you what your brain hasn't fully figured out yet.

Dealing with triggers doesn't mean avoiding life altogether. Instead, gather tools to manage your reaction. Here are some strategies:

- **Pause and breathe.** When you feel triggered, take a moment to focus on your breathing. Inhale deeply for four seconds, hold it for four, and exhale slowly for six. This helps calm your nervous system.
- **Name what you're feeling.:** Saying to yourself, "I feel anxious" or "I'm overwhelmed right now," can help you step back from the emotion and see it more clearly.

- **Ground yourself.** Use the 5-4-3-2-1 sensory method to draw attention to the present moment.

Triggers might not always feel so intense. The more you work on recognizing and processing them, the less power they'll have over you. Journaling, somatic exercises, and therapy are great ways to desensitize yourself to these emotional landmines over time.

The Role of Support in Trigger Management

You don't have to manage triggers on your own. A supportive environment makes a huge difference.

Talk to your family about what you're going through. Let them know what triggers you and how they can help, such as giving you space or talking things through calmly. If it's hard to open up, writing them a note can be a good first step.

You can also turn to people outside your family, like a school counselor, a trusted teacher, or a support group. Community resources (therapy apps, crisis hotlines, or local programs) are also available to help.

Handling triggers takes time, and it's okay if you don't always get it right. The important thing is that you're taking steps to understand yourself better and build a life where triggers don't control your every move.

BUILDING YOUR EMOTIONAL TOOLBOX

Think of your emotional toolbox as your personal survival kit for navigating tough feelings. You need to have a set of tools you can count on when you're feeling stressed, overwhelmed, angry, or unsteady. Just like you'd use a hammer to fix something at home, your emotional tools are practical strategies to help you handle life's challenges—especially when dealing with the effects of trauma. This toolbox gives you a way to feel more in control, stay calm, and handle emotions in a healthy way.

Creating Your Toolbox

Your emotional toolbox is unique to you. Find somatic techniques that help you feel safe and grounded, especially when life feels overwhelming. Since everyone's needs are different, it's important to explore and choose tools that fit you best.

Simple grounding techniques, such as 5-4-3-2-1 and grounded breathing, are a great place to start. These actions anchor you in the here and now, helping you feel more stable and less caught up in overthinking or emotional overwhelm.

Breathing exercises, such as deep belly and box breathing, are essential tools. These techniques give you something to focus on besides your stress and triggers and help you feel more relaxed.

Personalizing Your Toolbox

Once you've gathered some tools, the next step is figuring out how and when to use them. Different situations call for different approaches, so it's helpful to have a mix of strategies ready.

For example, if you're feeling nervous before a test or a social event, grounding or deep breathing might be your go-to tools. But if you're feeling angry or frustrated, physical movement—like stretching, walking, or even squeezing a stress ball—can help release built-up tension. Recognizing your emotions and how they show up in your body can help you choose the right tool for the moment.

The more you use these tools, the better you'll get at knowing what works for you. If tough conversations make you anxious, have a breathing or grounding technique ready. If certain memories feel overwhelming, try combining grounding with another activity that makes you feel safe, like journaling or listening to calming music.

Growing Your Toolbox

Your emotional toolbox isn't set in stone—it's meant to grow and change with you. As you learn more about yourself and your emotions, you'll discover new tools that fit your needs. Maybe you'll try mindfulness techniques, guided meditations, or creative outlets like art or music.

It's also important to check in with yourself regularly. Which tools are working well? Which might need some tweaking? If something isn't as effective anymore, it's okay to let it go and try something new. Keeping your toolbox fresh and personalized ensures it stays a reliable resource for handling stress and emotions in any situation.

Having an emotional toolbox gives you the confidence to face challenges with a plan. Even when life gets tough, you'll know you've got what it takes to handle it.

CREATING A SAFE SPACE FOR HEALING

Healing starts with having a safe space, a sanctuary where you feel secure, calm, and in control. It doesn't have to just be a physical spot; it can also be an emotional space that allows you to relax and be yourself. Whether it's your bedroom, a cozy corner, or even an inner feeling you carry with you, a safe space helps you recharge and focus on your healing.

What Makes a Space "Safe"?

A safe space is about feeling protected from judgment and stress. It's a place where you can let your guard down, whether through physical adjustments—like soft blankets, calming lights, and decluttered surroundings—or emotional boundaries, like setting rules with family about uninterrupted time for yourself. The goal is to create an environment that feels personal and soothing.

Balance Is Essential

While your safe space is a tool for healing, it's not a place to hide from the world. Use it to recharge and practice self-care, but also make time to engage with friends, family, and your community. Balance ensures your safe space supports your growth rather than keeping you isolated.

Consistency Builds Comfort

Safe spaces work best when they're reliable. Set routines to make your space familiar and comforting, such as lighting a candle, playing soft music, or practicing a calming ritual when you enter. These small habits create a sense of predictability that helps you feel grounded.

Add personal touches like calming colors, photos of loved ones, or items that make you happy. This isn't about following someone else's idea of comfort—it's about what works for you. Designing your safe space also allows you to reclaim control, empowering you to take charge of your healing.

EMPOWERING TEENS WITH TRAUMA-INFORMED CARE

Empowerment is about taking back control and feeling confident in your ability to heal—it's like stepping into the driver's seat of your life after tough experiences. In trauma recovery, empowerment equips you with tools and support to make decisions, set boundaries, and recognize your strengths. It starts with small, realistic goals, like practicing a somatic exercise daily or speaking up about your feelings. Each goal you accomplish, no matter how small, builds your belief in your ability to handle challenges.

Recovery is your journey, and autonomy plays a big role in making it meaningful. Autonomy means making choices that feel right for you—whether it's deciding which coping strategies to use or saying "no" to things that don't feel safe. By taking charge of your healing, you create a path that feels personal and empowering, helping you regain a sense of control over your life.

The Power of Support Systems

Empowerment doesn't mean going it alone. Having the right people in your corner makes all the difference.

- **Family Support:** Family can lift you up by offering a listening ear or helping with self-care routines. If they don't understand what you need, it's okay to communicate and ask for support.
- **Friends and Peers:** Your friends can be a cheer squad, offering encouragement, laughter, or a safe space to share your feelings. Peer support groups can also help you connect with others who get what you're going through.
- **Therapists and Counselors:** Your therapist or counselor can play a big role in supporting you by creating a safe, predictable, and respectful space just for you. They are there to teach you helpful coping techniques like somatic exercises, grounding practices, or mindful breathing, giving you a judgment-free zone to explore and work through tough feelings. By really listening to what you need and using a trauma-informed approach, they help build trust and empower you to take charge of your own healing journey.

Download your interactive chapter worksheets *NOW* to apply these techniques, track your progress, and build real emotional resilience—one step at a time.

SCAN QR CODE FOR DOWNLOADABLE WORKSHEETS

INTERACTIVE WORKSHEET

Use this worksheet to track your daily progress with somatic exercises, journaling prompts, and trauma-informed techniques. Fill it out at the end of each day or week to reflect on your journey and adjust as needed.

Daily Somatic Exercise Tracker

Date	Exercise Performed	Duration	How Did You Feel After	Beginning HRV	Ending HRV
Example: Monday	Gentle stretching and shaking	10 minutes	Felt less tense		
Tuesday					
Wednesday					
Thursday					
Friday					
Saturday					
Sunday					

Journaling Prompt Tracker

Instructions: Write down your prompt and a quick summary of your response.

Date	Prompt Used	Key Reflection/Insight
Example: Monday	What does safety feel like to me?	Safety means being calm and supported.
Tuesday		
Wednesday		
Thursday		
Friday		
Saturday		
Sunday		

Trauma-Informed Techniques Log

Instructions: Log specific techniques you used to manage triggers or emotional distress.

Date	Techniques Used	Trigger/Emotion Addressed	Effectiveness (1-5)	Beginning HRV	Ending HRV
Example: Monday	Grounding breath	Anxiety	4		
Tuesday					
Wednesday					
Thursday					
Friday					
Saturday					
Sunday					

End of Week Review:

1. What somatic exercises or techniques worked best for you this week?

_____

_____

2. Were there any moments when you felt a significant emotional or physical shift?

_____

_____

_____

3. What challenges did you face, and how did you address them?

_____

_____

_____

4. What's one goal you want to focus on next week?

_____

_____

Notes or Additional Thoughts:

_____

_____

_____

_____

Keep this tracker as a record of your healing journey. Celebrate the small wins and remind yourself of the progress you're making!

6

LONG-TERM STRATEGIES FOR WELL-BEING

"It's not about perfect. It's about effort. And when you bring that effort every single day, that's where transformation happens."

— JILLIAN MICHAELS

Sticking to a wellness routine can feel like a lot. Between school, friends, extracurriculars, and just trying to chill, it's easy to let self-care slip to the bottom of your to-do list. But a sustainable routine is one that works for you, not the other way around.

Think of your wellness routine as a marathon, not a sprint. Sure, you can go all out for a week, but if it's not manageable long-term, you'll burn out faster than you can say, "I'll start again Monday." A sustainable routine is flexible—it adapts when life gets busy. It's also consistent, helping you build habits that stick. The goal is to feel good, not overwhelmed.

Consistency is important, but some days feel "off." Maybe you had a tough test or stayed up too late binging a new show (we've all been there). The trick is knowing when to push through and when to cut yourself some slack. If you miss a day, don't sweat it. Just pick back up where you left off.

CREATE YOUR WELLNESS PLAN

So, are you ready to craft a wellness plan that's as unique as you are? Let's break it down:

Step 1: Identify Your Key Wellness Components

Ask yourself, "What makes me feel good?" Maybe it's moving your body, journaling, practicing somatic exercises, or spending time outside. Start with two to three things that you know will help you reset.

Step 2: Align With Your Goals

What's the goal you're going for? More energy? Less stress? Better focus? Pick routines that match your goals. For example, if you're feeling drained, add a short daily stretch or a quick breathing exercise to your mornings.

Step 3: Keep It Real

Set a schedule that fits your life. If mornings are chaotic, try adding wellness practices to your evenings instead. The idea is to work it into your routine, not disrupt it.

Even the best routines can get a little blah over time, so how do you keep things fresh and fun?

Grab a journal or an app and track your progress. Seeing those streaks build up can be a major confidence boost. Reward yourself when you hit milestones, like treating yourself to something you love after sticking to your routine for a month.

Also, try a new yoga flow, listen to a different playlist, or journal with a fun new prompt. Variety keeps things interesting and stops your routine from feeling like a chore.

ADAPTING SOMATIC PRACTICES OVER TIME

Life changes, and so do you. What worked for you a year ago might not align with who you are now. That's normal! Evolving your wellness practices is about staying connected to yourself and ensuring your routines grow with you. Think of it like updating your playlist—swapping out those old songs for new bangers that fit your current mood.

Your needs, goals, and energy levels shift as you grow. Maybe you're starting at a new school, dealing with an unexpected event, or feeling different about what you want out of life. Changing your wellness routine keeps it fresh and relevant so it always supports the current you.

When you were younger, your idea of self-care might have been grabbing a snack and watching cartoons. Now, it might include journaling, doing a grounding exercise, or going for a walk. Your body, mind, and self-care should also change as you mature. Your personal growth will require you to level up.

So, how do you modify somatic practices in response to changing circumstances, such as transitioning to a new school or dealing with life events?

Adjust Intensity and Frequency

You feel like a rockstar some weeks, and other weeks, not so much. That's okay. You can dial things up or down depending on what's happening in your life. Feeling drained? Do a shorter, gentler version of your somatic practices. Do you have extra energy? Go for something more dynamic, like dancing or jogging.

Incorporate New Techniques

Don't be afraid to try something new! Explore other options if your old routine isn't working anymore. Maybe swap out your usual stretches for a yoga flow or trade your journaling time for mindful coloring. Keep experimenting until you find what clicks.

The Concept of Seasonal Adjustments

Ever notice how your mood and energy change with the seasons? That's your body responding to nature—it's pretty cool. Adapting your practices to the seasons can make them even more effective.

In winter, you might focus on cozy indoor practices like deep breathing or gentle stretches. Come summer, you could take it outside with walks, hikes, or grounding exercises in the grass. Let the seasons inspire your routine.

Somatic therapy has a ton of different practices to try, from breathwork to body awareness techniques. Keep an open mind and explore what's out there. You never know when you'll discover a technique that feels like a winner.

Also, this might sound fancy, but workshops, webinars, or even online tutorials can teach you new techniques and help you deepen your practice. They're a great way to learn from others and connect with people who are into the same stuff.

EMBRACE A HOLISTIC LIFESTYLE

Ever heard the phrase "mind, body, and soul"? That's the essence of a holistic lifestyle—taking care of all the parts of you so they work together in harmony. It's not about being perfect or following strict rules. It's about finding balance and living in a way that makes you feel good from the inside out. Let's see how you can make this your own.

A holistic lifestyle means looking at your well-being; your physical, mental, and emotional health are all connected. If one part is out of whack, it can mess with the others. For example, when you're stressed, your body might feel tense, or you might struggle to focus. A holistic approach helps you care for all these pieces to feel balanced and strong.

Below are the components of a holistic lifestyle:

- **Physical Health:** Moving your body, eating well, and getting enough rest
- **Mental Health:** Keeping your mind sharp and managing stress
- **Emotional Health:** Understanding and expressing your feelings in healthy ways

So, how do you combine somatic practices with other wellness activities?

Nutrition and Somatic Health

What you eat fuels everything—your body, brain, and mood. Pairing good nutrition with somatic practices can be a big help. For example, eating nutrient-rich foods like fruits, veggies, and whole grains can boost your energy for movement-based exercises. Feeling sluggish? A balanced snack like nuts or yogurt can help you recharge before diving into a somatic routine.

Impact of Sleep on Emotional Balance

Sleep is everything. When you're rested, keeping your emotions in check and focusing on somatic practices is easier. Make sleep a priority.

Mindfulness and Holistic Health

Mindfulness isn't just about meditating; it's about being present in whatever you're doing. You can turn any moment into a mindfulness practice—eating breakfast, brushing your teeth, or walking to class. Being mindful helps you notice how you're feeling physically and emotionally, which is a huge part of holistic health.

Daily Routines for Holistic Health

Start small. Here's an example:

- **Morning:** Stretch for five minutes and set a positive intention for the day.
- **Afternoon:** Eat a nourishing lunch and take a mindful break to check in with yourself.
- **Evening:** Do a quick body scan before bed to release any tension.

Find the sweet spot. Push yourself when needed (like studying for a test), but also make time for fun (like hanging out with friends) and relaxation (like chilling with a good book). When you balance these, life feels more manageable and enjoyable.

SETTING AND ACHIEVING WELLNESS GOALS

When you want to feel your best—physically, mentally, and emotionally—having clear goals is like having a map for your journey. Wellness isn't a destination; it's a journey toward a healthier, happier you. Let's talk about how to set goals that work and how to stick to them without feeling overwhelmed.

Think of your wellness goals as a playlist for your life. Each goal is a song that gets you closer to the vibe you want—more energy, less stress, or just feeling good in your skin. Goals give you direction and keep you motivated, even on tough days.

Have you ever heard of SMART goals? They're a super simple way to make sure your goals are clear and doable:

- **Specific:** Be clear about what you want to achieve.
- **Measurable:** Find a way to track your progress.
- **Attainable:** Keep it realistic—no need to aim for the moon.
- **Relevant:** Make sure it connects to what's important to you.
- **Time-bound:** Set a deadline or timeline to keep you on track.

For example, instead of saying, "I want to be healthier," try, "I'll do a 10-minute somatic stretching routine three times a week for the next month."

So, how do you create effective wellness goals?

Define Specific, Measurable Goals

Start with what you want to feel. Do you want more energy? Less stress? Once you've nailed that, think about how you'll get there. If your goal is to manage stress, you could commit to practicing mindful breathing for five minutes a day.

Create Actionable Plans

Break your goal into bite-sized steps. Let's say your goal is to drink more water. Your action plan might look like this:

- Carry a reusable water bottle every day.
- Drink one glass of water before each meal.
- Set a phone reminder to drink water every two hours.

Find an Accountability Partner

Teaming up with a friend, family member, or mentor can keep you on track. They can cheer you on, check in with you, and maybe even join you in your wellness practices. You could also use apps or online groups to share progress and tips. Knowing someone has your back makes it easier to stay committed.

Reassess Goals Regularly

Life is unpredictable, and that's okay. Goals aren't set in stone—they're more like guideposts. Check in with yourself regularly to see if your goals still fit. Maybe you need to tweak your routine or focus on a new priority.

Adapt Goals to Life Changes

Got a big change coming up, like starting a new school or dealing with a busy schedule? Adjust your goals to match your new reality. For example, switch from a 30-minute workout to a quick 5-minute stretch if you're swamped with homework.

Measure Progress and Celebrate Success

Imagine playing a video game but never seeing your score. Pretty boring, right? Tracking your progress in your wellness journey shows you how far you've come, keeps you motivated, and helps you figure out what's working and what's not.

Measuring your progress is crucial. Why? Because when you see improvement—whether it's feeling less stressed, sleeping better, or nailing a new somatic exercise—it boosts your confidence. Plus, it's a chance to see where to switch things up.

Journal to Find Your Emotional Calm

Life can get messy—stress can make your head feel like it's spinning. That's where journaling comes in. It's a way to untangle the thoughts and emotions that swirl in your mind and connect them with what's happening in your body. Think of your journal as your personal space—no filters, no judgment, just you.

Journaling helps you figure out how you feel and why. Maybe you start with, "I feel off today," but as you write, you realize you're anxious about a test or upset about a comment someone made. Writing turns the chaos into something you can actually work with. Plus, it's a powerful partner for somatic practices.

After a somatic exercise, jot down how your body feels. Did deep breathing ease that knot in your stomach? Did grounding help slow your racing heart? Over time, you'll notice patterns, such as how mindful walking boosts your mood or a body scan melts away tension in your shoulders. Writing about these experiences creates a "cheat sheet" for what works to calm you down and handle stress.

Simple Journaling Tips

Journaling doesn't have to mean writing pages every day. It can be quick and flexible:

- Use a notebook or a journaling app like Daylio (for quick mood tracking) or Day One (for photos and notes).
- Keep it short. Write just a few sentences about how you feel or what's on your mind.
- Add prompts to get started, like:
- "What's been on my mind, and how does it make me feel?"

- "Where do I feel stress in my body?"
- "What's one thing I'm proud of today?"

Why It Works

Combining journaling with somatic practices gives your body and emotions a voice. By reflecting on what calms you or triggers stress, you'll become more self-aware. It may help you feel better in the moment, but it will also help you understand and manage your emotions long-term. The more you practice, the more in tune you'll be with yourself.

Make It a Habit

Journaling doesn't have to take a lot of time. Set aside five minutes when you feel most relaxed—maybe before bed or after school. Pair it with something you already do, like sipping a drink or settling into bed. Find a cozy spot, keep your journal nearby, and make it a daily habit. Those small moments can make a huge difference in handling life's ups and downs.

SELF-ASSESSMENT CHECKLISTS

Create a simple checklist to rate your feelings in areas like stress, focus, or energy. Do this weekly and compare your results. Seeing improvements, even small ones, can be super motivating.

Every time you hit a milestone, such as sticking to your routine for a week or feeling calmer during a stressful moment, celebrate it!

- Treat yourself to your favorite snack.
- Share your win with a friend or family member.
- Do a mini happy dance (because you deserve it).

Celebrating helps you feel good about your progress. Give yourself a high five and say, "I'm crushing this!" That positive vibe can keep you going, even on tough days. Take a few minutes each day to think about what you're grateful for. You can write it down or reflect on it mentally.

Focusing on the good stuff rewires your brain to notice more positives in your life. It's like planting seeds of happiness that grow stronger every day.

TOOLS AND RESOURCES TO SUPPORT HEALING JOURNEY

Life can get overwhelming sometimes, and having the right tools can make all the difference. Whether you're navigating tough emotions, trying to manage stress, or just looking to stay on top of your wellness game, these resources are here to support you. From apps to wearables and everything in between, let's explore some handy options to make your healing journey smoother and more empowering.

Digital Tools

We're all glued to our phones anyway, so why not use them for something that helps?

Meditation and Breathing Apps

Apps like Headspace, Calm, or Breathwrk guide you through calming breathing exercises and mindfulness practices. They're like having a stress coach in your pocket. Imagine taking a quick five-minute breather before that big test or during a rough day.

Mood Tracking Apps

Have you ever wondered why some days feel harder than others? Apps like Daylio or Moodfit let you track your daily emotional spot patterns and see what's working for you. It's a cool way of keeping a diary that is less time-consuming.

Mindfulness Reminders

Set up reminders on your phone to take a quick, mindful break. Maybe it's a reminder to stretch, do a grounding exercise, or take a few deep breaths. These tiny pauses can keep you from feeling completely fried.

Journaling Apps

Apps like Journey or Reflect give you space to unload your thoughts and feelings. They even toss in prompts to help you reflect. It's digital so that no one can snoop through your entries.

Sleep Support Apps

Struggling with sleep? Apps like Sleep Cycle or Insight Timer have relaxing sounds, sleep stories, and even white noise to help you drift off. Because let's face it, a good night's sleep can make or break the next day.

Wearable Technology

Wearables can be your new BFFs for those of you who love gadgets.

Smartwatch Alerts

Got a smartwatch? Set up alerts for breathing exercises or stress check-ins. It's a subtle way to stay on track without drawing attention.

Heart Rate Monitors

Are you feeling anxious but not sure why? Wearable heart rate monitors can clue you in. If your heart rate spikes, it's a signal to pause and do something calming, like deep breathing.

Sleep Trackers

Tools like FitBit or Oura Ring track your sleep patterns and show how well you recover. Seeing the data can motivate you to stick to healthier sleep habits because late-night scrolling isn't doing you any favors.

On-the-Go Support Tools

Quick support can make a huge difference when you're out and about.

Guided Visualization Videos

Bookmark or download calming visualization videos on YouTube. Think peaceful forests, ocean waves, or even a comforting voice guiding you through a moment of calm. They're perfect for when stress hits.

Portable Music Playlists

Create playlists that match your vibe—calming tunes for when you're stressed and upbeat tracks for when you need a mood boost. Platforms like Spotify or Apple Music have many options, or you can make your own. Bonus tip: Noise-canceling headphones make this even better.

Quick Access to Crisis Hotlines

Save important hotline numbers in your phone, like the Crisis Lifeline at 800-273-TALK (8255), or just text or call 988 anytime you need support. Having these contacts ready means help is always just a call or text away when you need it most. It's one of those things you hope you'll never need, but it's better to have it just in case. Sometimes, knowing help is just a call or text away can be a huge relief.

These tools aren't here to "fix" you because there's nothing wrong with needing support. They're here to help you feel more in control, stay grounded, and keep making progress. So, what's one tool you'd like to try first? Whether it's an app, a wearable, or a playlist, start small and see how it makes a difference.

Download your interactive chapter worksheets *NOW* to apply these techniques, track your progress, and build real emotional resilience—one step at a time.

SCAN QR CODE FOR DOWNLOADABLE WORKSHEETS

INTERACTIVE WORKSHEET

This worksheet is designed to help you track your journey with somatic exercises, journaling prompts, and strategies for long-term well-being. Use it daily or weekly to reflect on your progress and identify areas for growth.

Daily Somatic Exercise Tracker

Date	Exercise Performed	Duration	How Did You Feel After?	Beginning HRV	Ending HRV
Example: Monday	Breathing exercises	10 minutes	Felt calmer and more focused		
Tuesday					
Wednesday					
Thursday					
Friday					
Saturday					
Sunday					

Journaling Prompt Tracker

Write down the prompt you used and summarize your thoughts or insights.

Date	Prompt Used	Key Reflection/Insights
Example: Monday	What does self-care mean to me?	Self-care means making time for rest.
Tuesday		
Wednesday		
Thursday		
Friday		
Saturday		
Sunday		

Well-Being Strategies Log

Document the long-term well-being strategies you're working on, their outcomes, and how they're helping you.

Date	Strategy Used	Goal	Outcome/Reflection
Example: Monday	Nightly journaling	Better sleep and clarity	Slept deeply, felt refreshed
Tuesday			
Wednesday			
Thursday			
Friday			
Saturday			
Sunday			

Reflection Questions

Use these questions at the end of the week to review your progress.

1. What somatic exercises felt most effective this week, and why?

SIMPLE SOMATIC THERAPY FOR TEENS | 143

2. How did journaling help you process your emotions or experiences?

_____

_____

_____

3. Which long-term well-being strategies are you finding most helpful?

_____

_____

_____

4. What challenges did you face, and how can you address them moving forward?

_____

_____

_____

5. What is one thing you're proud of from this week?

_____

_____

_____

Gratitude and Celebration

End your week by writing down three things you're grateful for and one way you plan to celebrate your progress.

Three things I'm grateful for:

1. _____
2. _____
3. _____
4. _____
5. _____

How I will celebrate my progress:

_____

_____

_____

_____

_____

7

ENGAGING PARENTS AND GUARDIANS

"When you support a child's emotional well-being, you give them the tools to navigate life with confidence."

— DR. BECKY KENNEDY

This chapter is specifically for parents and guardians, and it highlights how you can actively support your teen's exploration of somatic therapy. Let's face it: Being a teen isn't easy—and neither is parenting. If your teen is diving into somatic therapy, you might be wondering how you can be part of their journey. And you should be: Your role is huge.

Somatic therapy is all about connecting the body and mind to deal with stress, emotions, and even trauma. It's not just some trendy thing—it's a proven way for teens to build resilience and find their balance. We know that teens thrive when they know their support system is solid. That's where you come in.

Whether you give them space to try out these techniques, cheer them on when they stick with a new habit, or even learn some of the exercises yourself, you can make their journey smoother and more meaningful.

UNDERSTANDING YOUR TEEN'S EMOTIONAL NEEDS

Understanding and supporting your teen's emotional health is crucial to adolescent parenting. As your teen goes through this stage's physical, mental, and emotional changes, their emotional needs can shift rapidly. The teenage years are marked by significant brain development, fluctuating hormones, and the search for independence, all of which can create emotional volatility. By recognizing these changes and knowing how to address them, you can provide the guidance and emotional support your teen needs to navigate this challenging time.

Adolescent Brain Development

As your teen navigates adolescence, it's essential to understand that their brain is still developing, particularly in areas responsible for emotional regulation and decision-making. The prefrontal cortex, which controls planning, impulse control, and understanding consequences, isn't fully matured until the mid-20s. This developmental stage often leads to emotional volatility since teens may struggle to regulate their emotions or see the bigger picture in stressful situations. Their brains are wired to react quickly to emotional stimuli, which sometimes results in overreactions or unpredictable behavior. Understanding these developmental changes helps parents recognize that many emotional challenges teens face are biological and temporary. Being patient and empathetic during these years will support their emotional growth.

Emotional Volatility in Teens

During adolescence, emotional extremes are common. Your teen might go from being completely happy to feeling overwhelmed or upset the next. This emotional volatility is often tied to the rapid hormonal and brain changes during this development phase. As they develop their identity, they may experience heightened sensitivity to peer opinions, self-image concerns, or pressure about future goals. These intense emotional shifts can sometimes confuse parents, but they are a normal part of growing up. Instead of reacting with frustration, approach these moments with understanding and patience. Recognizing that these emotional highs and lows are part of the process can help you provide the support your teen needs to navigate them.

Identify Emotional Needs

Identifying your teen's emotional needs can sometimes feel like a guessing game, but some tools and strategies can help. One approach is to monitor changes in behavior, mood, and interactions with others. It may indicate emotional distress if your teen suddenly withdraws from social activities or becomes more irritable. Using open-ended questions like, "How are you feeling today?" or "What's been on your mind lately?" allows you to tap into their emotional world and gain insight into their needs. Creating a "mood journal" can also help them track their emotions and identify patterns. By consistently checking in and observing their emotional state, you can better understand what they're going through and offer the proper support.

OBSERVATIONAL TECHNIQUES FOR PARENTS

One of the most effective ways to understand your teen's emotional needs is through careful observation. Pay attention to what they say and their nonverbal cues—body language, facial expressions, and tone of voice. Sometimes, teens may not be ready to verbalize their feelings, but their actions or behaviors can provide valuable insight into what they're experiencing. If you notice that your teen is more withdrawn, acting out, or showing signs of anxiety or anger, it's important to approach them in a non-judgmental way. For instance, instead of asking, "What's wrong with you?" try saying, "I've noticed you've been quieter lately. Is there anything you want to talk about?" This approach opens the door for dialogue without putting pressure on them to explain immediately.

Encouraging Emotional Expression

Helping your teen express their emotions is key to nurturing their emotional health. Encourage them to talk about their feelings, but also provide opportunities to express themselves in other ways. Some teens may find it easier to express their emotions through creative outlets like writing, drawing, or music. Others might benefit from physical activities like sports, dance, or yoga, which allow them to release pent-up energy and tension. By providing a range of options for emotional expression, you empower your teen to process their feelings in ways that feel comfortable to them. This helps them develop emotional resilience and a healthier relationship with their emotions.

COMMUNICATING EFFECTIVELY WITH TEENS

Effective communication is the foundation of any strong relationship, especially for parents and teens. As your teen navigates a world filled with new challenges and emotions, it's crucial to create an open, understanding space where they feel comfortable sharing their thoughts and feelings. How we communicate—whether through active listening, empathy, or even technology—can significantly influence the quality of these conversations. Adopting strategies that promote empathy, openness, and mutual respect can bridge the gap between generations and strengthen your trust and connection with your teen.

Active Listening Skills

Effective communication starts with listening—and I mean listening, not just hearing words. This requires being present in the conversation. When your teen speaks, put down your phone, make eye contact, and give them your full attention. Avoid interrupting, even if you feel like you have the perfect piece of advice to offer. Instead, focus on understanding their point of view and then respond thoughtfully. This creates a safe environment where your teen feels heard and valued, which is necessary for maintaining a strong, open relationship.

You can also use active listening techniques, like summarizing your teen's words, to ensure you're on the same page. Phrases like, "It sounds like you're feeling frustrated because…" show your teen you're genuinely engaged in understanding their experience. This helps avoid misunderstandings and builds empathy in the process.

Nonverbal Communication Cues

Body language plays a huge role in communication. How you sit, your facial expressions, and even your voice can either support or undermine your message. If you want your teen to feel comfortable sharing, ensure your body language is open and non-judgmental. Avoid crossing your arms, rolling your eyes, or raising your voice. Instead, lean in slightly, nod occasionally, and keep your tone calm and reassuring.

These subtle nonverbal cues can create an environment where your teen feels safe to talk without fear of being dismissed or judged. Your teen will also learn to read your cues, and this mutual understanding can foster more meaningful exchanges.

Empathetic Responses

When your teen shares something personal or challenging, respond with empathy rather than jumping straight into problem-solving. Acknowledge how they're feeling before offering advice or solutions. For example, saying, "I can see why you'd feel that way," or "That must be tough; I understand why you're upset," helps validate their emotions. Empathetic responses let your teen know that their feelings are heard and understood.

Remember, empathy doesn't always mean agreeing with your teen's point of view; it's about respecting their emotional experience. This validation strengthens trust and fosters a deeper sense of connection.

Acknowledging a Teen's Emotional Experiences

Your teen is navigating many emotions, which may be difficult to process. When you validate their feelings—whether sad, angry, or stressed—you show them that their emotions are real and worthy of attention. Sometimes, teens want to know that their emotions matter and that they're not alone in dealing with them.

Instead of brushing off their feelings with phrases like, "It's not that big a deal," acknowledge their experience. Try saying something like, "I see that this is important to you," or "It makes sense that you'd feel this way right now." This approach can help reduce your teen's emotional intensity and create space for a more constructive conversation.

Open-Ended Questioning Techniques

To encourage deeper dialogue, avoid asking yes-or-no questions that might shut down a conversation. Instead, ask open-ended questions that invite your teen to share their thoughts and feelings. Instead of asking, "Did you have a good day at school?" try, "What was the best part of your day at school?" or "How did that situation make you feel?"

Open-ended questions create a platform for your teen to express themselves more fully. This kind of questioning encourages reflection and helps uncover more about what's going on in their world. It's not about getting the "right" answer but giving your teen the space to speak freely and honestly.

Dialogue Starters for Difficult Conversations

There will be moments when you need to talk about tough topics—relationships, mental health, or something else weighing on your teen. These conversations can be intimidating, but the proper dialogue starters can set the tone for a productive exchange. Instead of diving straight into the issue, try easing in with something like, "I've noticed you seem a bit off lately. Want to talk about it?" or "It seems like something's been bothering you. How can I help?"

These questions show your teen that you care and are willing to listen rather than coming off as interrogating or judgmental. The goal is to create an atmosphere of openness where your teen feels safe sharing their thoughts without feeling pressured to do so.

Using Messaging Apps for Check-ins

In today's digital world, technology can be both a challenge and a tool for communication. Messaging apps can offer a low-pressure way to check in with your teen throughout the day. A simple "How's your day going?" or "Anything on your mind?" sent via text or instant message can open the door for more meaningful conversations later. Texting also allows your teen to communicate without feeling the stress of a face-to-face conversation, especially if they're dealing with something sensitive.

However, using this tool wisely is important—avoid using digital messaging as a substitute for in-person conversations. While texting is a helpful way to stay connected, nothing beats the depth and connection of face-to-face talks.

Balancing Screen Time With Face-to-Face Interactions

Problems can arise when technology starts to replace real conversations. While messaging apps are useful, making time for face-to-face interactions is essential, where you can read each other's body language and truly connect. Make it a priority to spend quality time together, whether it's through family meals, walks, or designated "phone-free" times.

This balance helps ensure that your teen doesn't retreat into digital spaces as their only form of communication. It also strengthens your relationship by reinforcing the importance of real-world interactions where both of you can truly listen and engage.

CREATING SUPPORTIVE FAMILY ENVIRONMENTS

A supportive home environment is like a safe zone where teens can feel understood, valued, and free to express themselves without fear of judgment or rejection. It's not just about avoiding conflict—it's about building a space filled with love, respect, and understanding. When teens know they can rely on their family for support, whether it's dealing with a tough day at school or navigating bigger emotional challenges, it gives them a strong foundation for growth and resilience.

Start by fostering open communication. Regular family discussions where everyone gets a chance to share their thoughts and feelings can make teens feel heard and appreciated. Adding bonding activities—like family meals, movie nights, or outdoor adventures—helps strengthen emotional connections and create moments of togetherness.

A supportive environment also includes being emotionally available, providing physical comfort, and maintaining a sense of stability. When teens feel secure at home, they're better equipped to face external pressures and handle life's challenges. Knowing they have a solid foundation of support gives them the confidence to grow and thrive emotionally.

Establishing House Rules for Respect and Kindness

Creating a positive atmosphere at home also involves setting clear expectations for behavior. While giving your teen some independence is important, setting house rules that promote respect and kindness helps establish a safe emotional space for everyone. These rules should be clear, consistent, and agreed upon by parents and teens. For example, rules like "We speak respectfully to each other" or "No yelling when discussing a disagreement" can prevent unnecessary conflict and promote healthy interaction. It's also helpful to frame rules positively—emphasizing what you want to see rather than focusing solely on what's not allowed.

Importance of Routine in Family Life

Consistency is key when it comes to creating a supportive environment. A stable routine gives your teen a sense of security and helps them manage stress. Having regular family meals, scheduled time for homework, and even consistent bedtimes can bring structure to your teen's day. While flexibility may be needed, knowing what to expect daily can ease anxiety and help your teen feel more grounded. A routine also creates opportunities for connection, such as family game nights or outdoor activities, which can strengthen bonds and create lasting memories.

Setting Realistic Expectations

Setting expectations that encourage growth and acknowledging your teen's challenges is important. Unrealistic or overly demanding expectations can lead to stress, anxiety, and a sense of failure, whereas setting reasonable goals can foster a sense of accomplishment. Focus on progress rather than perfection, and remember that mistakes are a natural part of learning and growing. Encouraging your teen to try their best while providing them with the tools and support they need to succeed can help them develop confidence and resilience. Balance high standards with positive reinforcement, and always celebrate their efforts, regardless of outcome. This approach allows your teen to feel empowered and supported as they navigate the ups and downs of adolescence.

Bridging the Generation Gap

How we think about mental health has shifted dramatically over the years, and we must recognize that generational differences play a significant role in how we approach these conversations. For parents, understanding this shift is key to supporting your teen. Older generations often view mental health through a more stigmatized lens, with less openness about struggles like anxiety, depression, or stress. Mental health should be "fixed" or ignored rather than discussed and understood. In contrast, today's younger generations are much more open about mental health issues. They're more likely to recognize the importance of mental well-being and seek help when needed.

Acknowledging your teen's perspective—while sharing your own experiences—can create a healthy space for open communication. This mutual understanding will help break down barriers and show your teen that you respect their feelings and experiences.

Engaging in Teen-Centric Activities

To truly connect with your teen, it's helpful to engage in activities they enjoy. This doesn't mean you need to become an expert in everything they're interested in, but taking the time to participate in their world shows that you care. Whether you play video games together, watch their favorite shows with them, or join in on creative hobbies, these activities provide an entry point into their lives.

This kind of engagement allows you to ask questions about what they enjoy and why, making it easier to discuss deeper issues. It also signals your teen that you're willing to step out of your comfort zone to be a part of their world.

Learning About Current Teen Culture

To build that bridge with your teen, take the time to learn about their world. This doesn't mean you need to become fully immersed in social media or adopt their slang, but understanding the cultural references, challenges, and trends they encounter can make conversations easier and more relevant. Explore what's trending in music, fashion, or social media platforms, and ask your teen to explain why they find these things appealing. It's not about keeping up but showing genuine interest in their perspective.

When you're informed, it becomes easier to understand what's influencing your teen, making it possible to offer more thoughtful guidance on how to deal with the pressures they face.

ADOPTING A GROWTH MINDSET

Parenting doesn't come with a one-size-fits-all guide. Parents must be open to new ideas and adaptable to changes in family dynamics. You may not always understand your teen's point of view right away, but adopting a growth mindset can make a difference. Instead of seeing challenges as barriers, view them as opportunities for growth for you and your teen.

Adaptability in your parenting style helps maintain a healthy, supportive relationship with your teen. Whether learning to communicate in a new way or embracing different approaches to handling stress, flexibility can help you navigate the evolving nature of your relationship with your teen.

Flexibility in Parenting Approaches

Sometimes, what worked in the past might not be effective in the present. You will need to be flexible in your parenting methods as you learn to respond to your teen's changing needs. If a traditional approach isn't working, consider adjusting your communication style, discipline methods, or expectations. Each teen is different, and being open to alternative strategies—like using positive reinforcement over strict rules—can help foster a deeper connection.

By showing that you're willing to listen and adapt to their needs, you encourage your teen to do the same, making your relationship more resilient in the long run.

Joint Participation in Workshops

One of the most effective ways to create lasting memories while strengthening your bond is to engage in joint learning experiences. Attend workshops, seminars, or support groups together. These activities can provide a safe space for you and your teen to explore mental health, communication strategies, and coping mechanisms. It allows you to learn from experts and share insights in a neutral setting.

Additionally, it can normalize difficult topics, making it easier for your teen to talk openly about what they're going through. These shared experiences can help you grow and evolve together, creating a more supportive family dynamic.

Family-Based Learning Experiences

Incorporating learning into your family life can be a game changer. Consider engaging in family-based experiences like meditation, yoga, or journaling. These activities encourage mindfulness and emotional awareness in a way that is accessible to everyone. Not only does it help with managing stress and emotions, but it also opens up opportunities for meaningful conversations about mental health.

Participating in these activities as a family creates a space where everyone's voice can be heard. It reinforces that you're all in this together, making it easier for your teen to open up about their experiences.

ENCOURAGE SOMATIC PRACTICES AT HOME

Integrating somatic practices into family life can be a powerful way to promote emotional well-being and strengthen connections within the family. As a parent, your involvement and support in these practices set the foundation for your teen to embrace mindfulness and body awareness as part of their daily routine. You can foster a home environment where emotional health is prioritized by modeling these practices, creating family-friendly activities, and celebrating progress.

Modeling Mindfulness Practices

Leading by example is one of the most powerful ways to support your teen's well-being. Your actions speak volumes

regarding somatic practices—mindfulness, breathing exercises, and body awareness. Incorporating these practices into your daily routine shows your teen that
taking care of your body and mind is a priority. Whether setting aside a few
minutes in the morning for meditation or practicing deep breathing when
stressed, your teen will see how these practices can help manage emotions and
stress. You don't need to be perfect, but the more consistent you are, the more
likely they'll want to join in and embrace these practices themselves.

Family Somatic Sessions

Making somatic practices a family activity can positively affect your relationship
and everyone's emotional health. You might start by scheduling family mindfulness sessions, such as doing a short meditation together in the evening or practicing gentle stretching before dinner. Doing this as a group normalizes the
practice and fosters a sense of togetherness. It's a chance to slow down as a family,
connect emotionally, and create a shared experience that promotes well-being.
These moments can help everyone unwind, reduce stress, and set the tone for
positive communication throughout the day.

Family Stretching Routines

Integrating somatic practices doesn't have to be complicated or time-consuming.
Try setting aside a few minutes daily to do simple stretching exercises as a family.
Whether in the morning to start the day or in the evening to wind down,
stretching together can be a fun and bonding experience. It doesn't have to be an
intense workout; gentle stretches to relieve tension and increase flexibility can be
enough. It's a great way to introduce the concept of listening to your body and
encouraging your teen to make physical awareness a part of their daily routine.

Group Breathing Exercises

Breathing exercises are another excellent way to integrate somatic practices into
family life. Group breathing exercises, such as deep belly breathing or the 4-7-8

technique, can quickly calm everyone's nerves, reduce stress, and bring a sense of mindfulness into the home. Set aside time as a family to do these exercises together, perhaps during a calm moment or even before a stressful event like a family meeting or school presentation. Practicing together creates a shared space where everyone can connect emotionally and mentally. These exercises help your teen learn emotional regulation and encourage a family culture of self-care.

Establishing Regular Practice Times

Consistency is key when it comes to somatic practices. Just as you might establish a bedtime routine or a weekly family dinner, consider setting regular times for mindfulness practices. Having a set routine—whether it's a morning breathing session, a quick stretch before bed, or a family meditation on the weekend—creates a sense of stability and reinforces the benefits of these practices. Making somatic exercises part of your daily or weekly routine helps your teen see them as a natural part of life rather than an occasional task. This consistency can make these practices more effective, leading to lasting emotional resilience and a stronger family bond.

Praise for Practice Efforts

Positive reinforcement goes a long way in motivating your teen to stick with somatic practices. Whether they join a family meditation session or take a moment to breathe when stressed, your support can make all the difference. Focus on their effort rather than the outcome, and celebrate the small steps they take towards integrating mindfulness into their routine. This positive feedback encourages your teen to continue practicing and helps them feel validated in their efforts, which is key to maintaining motivation over time.

Celebrating Milestones in Emotional Growth

Somatic practices are not just about physical exercises—they're about emotional growth, too. Celebrate their milestones as your teen begins to feel the benefits of mindfulness and body awareness. Whether it's their increased ability to manage stress or their greater emotional awareness, acknowledging these improvements reinforces the importance of their practice. You could celebrate with a small treat, a family outing, or an expression of pride in their progress. Celebrating these milestones helps keep your teen motivated, encourages their continued emotional development, and reminds them that their efforts are paying off.

Resilience-Building Activities

Building emotional resilience is an ongoing process, and as a parent, you can play a pivotal role in this development. Encouraging your teen to face challenges head-on—while providing a supportive and non-judgmental space—helps them develop coping skills for managing stress, disappointment, or failure. Activities like problem-solving together, learning mindfulness techniques, or participating in resilience-building exercises (such as journaling or gratitude practices) can help your teen build emotional strength. Celebrate their progress in overcoming a difficult situation or learning to manage their emotions better. By supporting your teen through these challenges, you help them grow into a more emotionally resilient and self-aware individual.

OVERCOMING PARENTAL SKEPTICISM

It's natural for parents to feel skeptical about somatic therapy, especially if it's unfamiliar. You may have questions about its effectiveness or how it fits into more traditional approaches to emotional health. After all, therapies like talk therapy or medication have been the standard for years, and somatic practices may seem unconventional in comparison. Some parents may worry that these practices are unproven or "too alternative" to be taken seriously. However, you should understand that somatic therapy is not just some trendy or vague technique—it's rooted in research and aims to help individuals access deeper emotional and physical connections, which can be transformative in healing.

Looking at the research supporting somatic practices can help ease concerns you may have. Studies have shown that somatic therapies, such as body-focused psychotherapy or trauma release exercises, can effectively reduce stress, anxiety, and trauma-related symptoms. Research highlights the connection between the mind and body, showing that physical tension is often linked to emotional blockages or trauma (Murnan 2023). For example, studies on trauma therapy usually focus on how the body stores emotional pain and how somatic techniques, like breathing exercises or movement, can release that tension, leading to emotional healing. This body-mind connection isn't just theoretical; it's a real and proven approach that can support emotional well-being in meaningful ways.

Hearing from other parents who have seen positive changes from somatic practices can be incredibly reassuring. Many parents report that their teens have benefited from the deeper emotional awareness and stress reduction that somatic therapy promotes. These real-world success stories show that somatic practices have made a tangible difference for many families, offering hope and encouragement for those who may be uncertain.

If you are still unsure about the benefits of somatic therapy, reading is a great way to learn more. Books that explore the science of trauma and healing through the body can help clarify the benefits of somatic approaches. Books like The Body Keeps the Score: Brain, Mind, and Body in the Healing of Trauma" – by Bessel van der Kolk, M.D. and Waking the Tiger: Healing Trauma" – by Peter A. Levine, Ph.D., will give you a deeper understanding of how somatic therapy works and explain why it's gaining recognition in emotional health.

In addition to reading, attending workshops or seminars on somatic practices can help you see these therapies in action and gain firsthand knowledge. Many therapists offer introductory workshops where you can learn basic somatic techniques like breathing exercises, grounding techniques, and movement practices. These sessions often provide an opportunity to ask questions, connect with other parents, and understand how somatic therapy can fit into your family's routine. Workshops also allow you to experience somatic practices in a safe, supportive environment, which can help ease any lingering doubts about their efficacy.

If you're still unsure, one of the best ways to address your concerns is by conversing with a trained somatic therapist. A professional can explain the specific benefits of somatic therapy, how it works, and why it might be a good fit for your teen. They can also offer a more personalized approach by discussing how somatic practices can address your teen's unique emotional needs. Direct consultation with a professional can help you feel more informed and confident in your decision. This open dialogue also allows you to ask any lingering questions, ensuring you fully understand the therapy before deciding whether it's right for your family.

ENGAGING EXTERNAL SUPPORT RESOURCES

Supporting your teen's emotional well-being involves working together with both family and external resources. While a strong foundation at home is crucial, sometimes teens feel more comfortable opening up to someone outside the family, like a counselor, therapist, or trusted adult. Encouraging your teen to engage with a therapist or join peer support groups can provide additional tools for coping and emotional expression. When we normalize seeking help, we show them it's okay to reach out when needed and reinforce that emotional support comes in many forms.

If your teen is already working with a mental health professional, consider discussing the potential benefits of somatic therapy in a collaborative meeting. By combining somatic practices with traditional therapy techniques, you, your teen, and their counselor can create a holistic approach that addresses both emotional and physical well-being. Collaboration between family members and profes-sionals often leads to the best outcomes, ensuring a tailored and integrative support system for your teen. With a diverse network of support, they'll have the resources needed to navigate challenges and thrive.

Download your interactive chapter worksheets _NOW_ to apply these techniques, track your progress, and build real emotional resilience—one step at a time.

SCAN QR CODE FOR DOWNLOADABLE WORKSHEETS

INTERACTIVE WORKSHEET

Here's a worksheet for tracking progress with somatic exercises, journaling prompts, and parenting techniques. Both parents and teens can use this to reflect on emotional growth and somatic practice over time.

Somatic Exercises

1. Exercises practiced today: (e.g., breathing exercise, body scan, stretching, grounding, yoga, etc.)

_____

_____

2. How long did you practice? (e.g., 10 minutes, 30 minutes)

_____

_____

3. How did your body feel before the practice? List any tension, discomfort, or emotional states you experienced before you started.

_____

_____

4. How did your body feel after the practice? Note any changes in physical tension, energy, or emotional state.

_____

_____

5. Did any thoughts or feelings come up during the practice? Did any emotions surface or thoughts arise?

_____

_____

6. Overall rating of the somatic practice today (1–5): (1 = No change, 5 = Significant positive change)

_____

_____

Journaling Prompts

1. How did you feel today, emotionally and physically? Use this prompt to reflect on your emotional and physical state throughout the day. What stood out?

_____

_____

2. What challenges did you face today? Identify any obstacles or emotional difficulties you encountered today and how you dealt with them.

_____

_____

3. How did you handle difficult emotions today? Reflect on how you managed stress, anxiety, or anger. Did somatic exercises or other techniques help?

_____

_____

4. What small victories or positive moments happened today? Recognize any successes or positive changes, no matter how small.

_____

_____

5. What are your goals for tomorrow regarding emotional health or somatic practice? (Set intentions for the next day.

_____

_____

Parenting Techniques

1. How did you practice active listening with your teen today? Give an example of how you showed empathy or validated their feelings.

_____

_____

2. Were there any opportunities for positive reinforcement today? What positive behaviors did you reinforce or encourage?

_____

_____

3. Did you spend time bonding or engaging with your teen today? Describe a moment of connection or shared activity.

_____

_____

4. Did you set or reinforce any house rules today that promote respect and kindness? How did you model or encourage respectful behavior in your home?

_____

_____

5. Were the expectations you set for your teen today realistic and balanced? Reflect on whether the goals set were achievable without overwhelming them.

_____

_____

6. Was there consistency in your home today regarding routines and structure? Did any part of your routine offer emotional stability or predictability for your teen?

_____

_____

Reflections

1. What did you learn about yourself today as a parent or part of the process?

_____

_____

2. Have you encountered obstacles while practicing somatic techniques or applying parenting strategies?

_____

_____

3. What are you looking forward to working on tomorrow?

_____

_____

Use this tracker to evaluate your growth, monitor changes, and reflect on how somatic practices and positive parenting strategies impact your emotional health and relationship with your teen. This will also help you stay accountable to the process and celebrate incremental progress over time.

SHARE THE POWER OF SOMATIC THERAPY

The skills you've picked up here will serve you throughout your entire life, and I hope you're going to feel a positive difference. I have no doubt that you'll go on to inspire others—but if you want an easy way to start doing that right now, all you have to do is leave a short review.

Simply by sharing your honest opinion of this book and a little about how you've been using it to improve your own experience, you'll inspire other people to investigate somatic therapy for themselves—and you'll show them exactly where they can find all the guidance they need to get started.

Thank you so much for your support. I'm excited for the future you have ahead of you, and I know you're going to inspire other people every step of the way.

Scan the QR Code below to leave your review on Amazon.

CONCLUSION

"You don't have to control your thoughts. You just have to stop letting them control you."

— DAN MILLMAN

If you've made it this far—congrats! Seriously, take a moment to appreciate the effort you've put into learning about somatic therapy and how it can help you take charge of your mental health. This book was about giving you real tools to make your life better, one breath, one stretch, and one mindful moment at a time.

Throughout these pages, we've explored how somatic therapy connects your mind and body in powerful ways. Whether you're dealing with anxiety, working through tough experiences, or just trying to feel more balanced, somatic practices can help. Techniques like grounding exercises, body scans, and mindful breathing give you practical ways to calm your mind, ease stress, and build emotional strength.

And here's the big takeaway: You can create resilience. Emotional resilience isn't something you're born with—it's something you build every day by showing up for yourself, even in small ways.

Emotional resilience helps you bounce back when life throws curveballs. It allows you to handle stress without shutting down and stay grounded when things feel overwhelming. By practicing the somatic exercises in this book regularly, you're training your body and mind to work together, making it easier to face challenges confidently.

Let's not forget the science we touched on: Your mind and body are always communicating. Somatic therapy taps into that connection to improve your mental health. Whether it's calming your nervous system, reducing physical tension, or boosting your focus, these techniques work because they honor how deeply your body and emotions are linked.

Remember the exercises we explored? From grounding techniques and body scans to mindful stretching and breathing routines, these are simple, practical tools you can use anytime, anywhere. The best part? They don't take much time or fancy equipment—just a willingness to tune in to yourself.

Here's the thing: Real change happens with consistency. You don't have to be perfect or do every exercise daily, but sticking with even one or two practices regularly can make a huge difference. Over time, these small habits can shift how you feel and handle life's ups and downs.

It's important to remember that you don't have to do this alone. Your parents, teachers, counselors, and friends can all be part of your support system. Share what you've learned, ask for help when needed, and encourage the people around you to join you in creating a healthier, more supportive environment.

To every teen reading this: This is *your* journey. You get to decide how to use the tools in this book. Try different exercises, mix things up, and determine what works best. Somatic therapy isn't one-size-fits-all—it's about discovering what feels right for your body and mind.

Somatic therapy is about building stronger, healthier communities. Imagine a world where schools, families, and neighborhoods prioritize emotional resilience and mental well-being. You can be part of this movement. Share what you've learned, join workshops, or even start conversations about somatic therapy in your community.

Your wellness journey doesn't end here. It's a lifelong process of learning, growing, and adapting. Somatic practices are tools you can carry as you navigate whatever comes next—high school, college, work, relationships, and beyond. Keep exploring, practicing, and believing in your ability to grow.

To the adults in the room: Your role is crucial. Teens need your support to explore and practice these techniques. Whether you encourage mindfulness at home, introduce somatic practices in schools, or simply listen with empathy, your actions can make a difference.

Finally, thank you for showing up for yourself and letting this book be part of your journey. I hope the tools and insights shared here make a positive difference in your life—and maybe even inspire you to help others.

You've got this. Here's to resilience, growth, and a life full of possibility.

NEUROSOMATIC RESOURCES

WEARABLE DEVICES FOR HEART RATE & HEALTH TRACKING

Apple Smart Watch

- Use: Tracks heart rate, HRV, activity, and stress levels to support overall wellness
- Where to Get: Available at Apple stores or online
- More Info: https://www.apple.com/watch

Oura Ring

- Use: Monitors HRV, sleep patterns, and recovery to optimize health and stress management
- Where to Get: Purchase online at Oura's website
- More Info: https://ouraring.com

Polar H10 Chest Strap

- Use: A highly accurate heart rate monitor for HRV and fitness tracking during exercise
- Where to Get: Available online or at fitness retailers
- More Info: https://www.polar.com

Whoop Strap

- Use: Monitors HRV, sleep, strain, and recovery to help optimize performance and wellness
- Where to Get: Subscription-based purchase online at Whoop's website
- More Info: https://www.whoop.com

JOURNALING APPS FOR TRACKING OUTCOMES OF SOMATIC THERAPY

Daylio

- Use: Combines mood tracking with micro-journaling. Teens can log their daily activities, feelings, and habits without needing to write extensively. A fun visual interface, customizable mood icons, and habit tracking make it easy and appealing.
- Platforms: iOS, Android

Journey

- Use: Cloud-sync journal with multimedia options (photos, videos, and audio). It includes prompts and mood tracking. Journey offers a polished interface and integration with Google Drive for easy access across devices.

- Platforms: iOS, Android, Desktop

Penzu

- Use: Private, password-protected journal with customization options and prompts. It is secure and easy to use with a focus on personal privacy.
- Platforms: iOS, Android, Web

Reflectly

- Use: AI-driven personal journal that helps track emotions and offers prompts to encourage reflection. Reflectly encourages mindfulness and positivity with a modern, sleek design.
- Platforms: iOS, Android

Grid Diary

- Use: Template-based journaling with questions and prompts in a grid format. This app simplifies journaling into quick, manageable sections, making it less intimidating.
- Platforms: iOS, Android

Moodpath

- Use: Combines mood tracking with journaling and mental health assessments. Moodpath offers insights into emotional well-being and encourages self-awareness.
- Platforms: iOS, Android

Day One

- Use: Highly versatile journaling app with multimedia capabilities, password protection, and customizable reminders. It allows creative freedom with options for photos and drawings, appealing to creative teens.
- Platforms: iOS, Android, Mac

Journey Cloud

- Use: Cross-platform journaling with multimedia capabilities and a strong focus on well-being. It is easy to integrate with other tools and features that promote positive habits.
- Platforms: iOS, Android, Web

Stoic

- Use: Combines journaling with mindfulness and stoic philosophy. Includes prompts and guided reflections. Stoic helps teens explore deeper thoughts and feelings in a structured, guided way.
- Platforms: iOS, Android

Presently

- Use: Gratitude-focused journaling with daily prompts. This app encourages positivity and mindfulness with a simple, distraction-free interface.
- Platforms: Android (iOS coming soon)

MOBILE APPS FOR HRV, BREATHING, AND STRESS MANAGEMENT

Elite HRV

- Use: Measures HRV and provides insights into stress and recovery
- Where to Get: Available on iOS and Android app stores
- More Info: https://elitehrv.com

HeartMath

- Use: Offers biofeedback for stress reduction and emotional regulation through HRV tracking
- Where to Get: Download from app stores or purchase paired devices on their website
- More Info: https://www.heartmath.com

iBreathe

- Use: Guides breathing exercises for relaxation and anxiety management
- Where to Get: Free on iOS and Android app stores
- More Info: https://ibreatheapp.com

Breathwrk

- Use: Provides guided breathing exercises to reduce stress, improve focus, and enhance relaxation
- Where to Get: Available on iOS and Android app stores
- More Info: https://www.breathwrk.com

Calm

- Use: Combines guided meditations, sleep stories, and relaxation techniques to reduce stress and anxiety
- Where to Get: Available on iOS and Android app stores
- More Info: https://www.calm.com

Insight Timer

- Use: Features a library of meditations, including breathing and mindfulness exercises, tailored to your needs
- Where to Get: Free on iOS and Android app stores
- More Info: https://www.insighttimer.com

Wearable Devices for Nervous System Regulation

Apollo Neuro

- Use: Delivers gentle vibrations to the skin to reduce stress and improve focus
- Where to Get: Order from Apollo Neuro's website
- More Info: https://apolloneuro.com

Sensate

- Use: A wearable device that uses low-frequency sound vibrations to calm the nervous system and enhance relaxation
- Where to Get: Purchase online at Sensate's website
- More Info: https://www.getsensate.com

VAGUS NERVE STIMULATION DEVICES

Nurosym

- Use: Non-invasive device that stimulates the vagus nerve through the ear for relaxation and stress relief
- Where to Get: Purchase online at Nurosym's website
- More Info: https://nurosym.com

Pulsetto

- Use: Wearable device providing cervical vagus nerve stimulation via the neck to reduce stress and anxiety
- Where to Get: Order online at Pulsetto's website
- More Info: https://pulsetto.com

Hoolest

- Use: Handheld device stimulates the vagus nerve to reduce anxiety and improve mood
- Where to Get: Available online at Hoolest's website
- More Info: https://hoolest.com

Truvaga Plus

- Use: Offers quick, gentle vagus nerve stimulation for stress relief
- Where to Get: Purchase online at Truvaga's website
- More Info: https://truvaga.com

Neuvana Xen

- Use: Headphones that deliver electrical micro-pulses to the left ear, targeting vagus nerve stimulation
- Where to Get: Purchase on Neuvana's website
- More Info: https://neuvanalife.com

gammaCore

- Use: Handheld device approved for treating cluster headaches through non-invasive vagus nerve stimulation
- Where to Get: Available with a prescription or online
- More Info: https://www.gammacore.com

TENS UNITS FOR VAGUS NERVE STIMULATION

TENS Units for taVNS

- Use: Adapted TENS units with ear clip electrodes for transcutaneous auricular vagus nerve stimulation (taVNS) to promote relaxation, reduce inflammation, and alleviate depression symptoms
- Where to Get: Purchase TENS units and specialized electrodes online or at medical retailers
- More Info: https://www.ncbi.nlm.nih.gov/pmc/articles/PMC5534856/

ADDITIONAL TOOLS FOR STRESS MANAGEMENT AND WELLNESS

Muse Meditation Headband

- Use: Provides real-time biofeedback during meditation to track and enhance relaxation
- Where to Get: Purchase online at Muse's website
- More Info: https://choosemuse.com

Somavedic Devices

- Use: Creates a field that mitigates EMF exposure and promotes physical and mental harmony
- Where to Get: Available online at Somavedic's website
- More Info: https://somavedic.com

Blue Light Blocking Glasses

- Use: Reduces exposure to blue light, improving sleep quality and reducing eye strain
- Where to Get: Available at various online and retail stores
- More Info: https://www.blublox.com

REFERENCES

4 techniques for practicing self-compassion. (2023, July 26). Cleveland Clinic. https://health. clevelandclinic.org/self-compassion

4 ways to boost your self-compassion. (2016, January 25). Harvard Health. https://www.health.harvard. edu/mental-health/4-ways-to-boost-your-self-compassion

Admin. (2024, December 13). Reichian Segmental Armouring Theory | Muscular Body Armour. Energetics Institute. https://energeticsinstitute.com.au/characterology/reichs-segmental-armouring-theory/

adminNHS. (2024, July 15). The ultimate guide to building a sustainable wellness routine. *INHS*. https://www.nhsinstitute.com/the-ultimate-guide-to-building-a-sustainable-wellness-routine/

Arootah. (2023, January 3). *18 sustainable wellness habits*. https://arootah.com/blog/health-and-wellbe ing/wellness/sustainable-wellness-habits/

Cherry, K. (2023, December 31). *5 key components of emotional intelligence*. Verywell Mind. https://www. verywellmind.com/components-of-emotional-intelligence-2795438

Chintapalli, S. (n.d.). *How do i tone my vagus nerve? 10 ways to heal it naturally*. MedicineNet. https:// www.medicinenet.com/how_do_i_tone_my_vagus_nerve/article.htm

Ehmke, R. (2023, April 14). *Tips for communicating with your teen*. Child Mind Institute. https://child mind.org/article/tips-communicating-with-teen/

Elmer, J. (2022, March 2). *What is a mental health crisis: Signs, causes, and how to get help*. Psych Central. https://psychcentral.com/health/what-is-a-mental-health-crisis

Exercise and stress: Get moving to manage stress. (2022, August 3). Mayo Clinic. https://www.mayoclinic. org/healthy-lifestyle/stress-management/in-depth/exercise-and-stress/art-20044469

Exercise for stress and anxiety. (n.d.). Anxiety and Depression Association of America. Retrieved January 20, 2025, from https://adaa.org/living-with-anxiety/managing-anxiety/exercise-stress-and-anxiety

Ginsburg, K. (2023, May 18). *7 expert tips for talking with teens*. Center for Parent and Teen Communication. https://parentandteen.com/keep-teens-talking-learn-to-listen/

Grounding techniques: Exercises for anxiety, ptsd, and more. (2019, May 24). Healthline. https://www. healthline.com/health/grounding-techniques

Guide to identifying emotional crisis. (n.d.). Loyola University Chicago - Wellness Center. https://www. luc.edu/wellness/mentalhealth/suicideprevention/guidetoidentifyingemotionalcrisis/

Harvard Health. (2024, April 3). Understanding the stress response. https://www.health.harvard.edu/ staying-healthy/understanding-the-stress-response

Hauser, R. (n.d.). *How you can repair your vagus nerves*. https://caringmedical.com/can-repair-vagus-nerves/

How to create a regular wellness routine. (2024, November 23). My Experiences. https://www.myexperiences.co.uk/how-to-create-a-regular-wellness-routine/

Kuhfuß, M., Maldei, T., Hetmanek, A., & Baumann, N. (2021). Somatic experiencing – effectiveness and key factors of a body-oriented trauma therapy: a scoping literature review. European Journal of Psychotraumatology, 12(1). https://doi.org/10.1080/20008198.2021.1929023

Laderer, A. (2024, January 19). *Vagus nerve exercises*. Charlie Health. https://www.charliehealth.com/post/vagus-nerve-exercises

Laoutaris, N. (2024, May 9). *Somatic therapy exercises and techniques*. First Session. https://www.firstsession.com/resources/somatic-therapy-exercises-techniques

Lea, S. (2023, April 11). Goleman's 5 Elements of EQ. Accipio. https://www.accipio.com/eleadership/personal-effectiveness/golemans-5-elements-of-eq/

Murnan, A. (2023, August 21). Can emotions be trapped in the body? What to know. https://www.medicalnewstoday.com/articles/emotions-trapped-in-the-body

Porrey, M. (2024, June 4). *Types and uses of somatic trauma therapy*. Verywell Health. https://www.verywellhealth.com/somatic-trauma-therapy-5218970

Raypole, C. (2024, January 29). *Grounding techniques: Exercises for anxiety, ptsd, and more*. Healthline. https://www.healthline.com/health/grounding-techniques

Resnick, Ariane. (2024, December 11). *What is somatic therapy?* Verywell Mind. https://www.verywellmind.com/what-is-somatic-therapy-5190064

Segal, J., Smith, M., & Robinson, L. (2018, November 2). *Improving emotional intelligence (Eq): Expert guide*. HelpGuide.Org. https://www.helpguide.org/mental-health/wellbeing/emotional-intelligence-eq

Somatic therapy for healing teen trauma. (2019, October 11). *Newport Academy*. https://www.newportacademy.com/resources/mental-health/somatic-therapy-healing-teen-trauma/

The Benefits of Somatic Therapy for Teenagers. (n.d.). Sue Redmond. https://www.sueredmond.com/pages/teen-somatic-therapy

The power of exercise for teens. (2018, September 4). Center for Parent and Teen Communication. https://parentandteen.com/stress-management-teens-exercise/

Wong, D. (2022, June 14). How to communicate with teenagers (11 actionable tips for parents). *Daniel Wong*. https://www.daniel-wong.com/2022/06/14/communicating-with-teens/

FUTURE BOOKS MARKETING PAGE

💬 **CONTINUE YOUR JOURNEY TO CALM**

If this book helped you feel more in control of your emotions and body, there's even more support available.

Explore the Full Simple Somatic Therapy for Teens Series

Alongside this main book, you'll find companion workbooks and guided journals designed to help you implement somatic therapy on a daily basis. With step-by-step exercises, reflection prompts, and calming check-ins, these tools support you in building emotional balance one day at a time.

📚 **Somatic Support for Every Stage of Life**

Looking for more? Holistic Harmony Publications offers somatic therapy books for all audiences. The *Simple Somatic Therapy Solution* book, workbook, and journal provide a complete step-by-step approach for adults seeking calm and nervous system regulation. For those wanting to integrate somatic practices with therapy techniques, *Integrative Somatic Therapy* combines the best of CBT, DBT, EMDR, and somatic therapy into one easy-to-follow guide.

Real Help for Real Teen Life

Whether you're navigating anxiety, trauma, mood swings, or stress, the Simple Somatic Therapy for Teens series is here to guide you—no pressure, no judgment, just simple tools that work.

Stay Connected with Holistic Harmony Publications

Find free resources, tools, and all available books at:

www.HolisticHarmonyPublications.com

Browse Our Books on Amazon

Check out the full series on the Holistic Harmony Publications Amazon author page:

amazon.com/Holistic-Harmony-Publications

www.ingramcontent.com/pod-product-compliance
Lightning Source LLC
Chambersburg PA
CBHW080957120626
46546CB00010B/2926